CHRISTMAS

CANDY ABBOTT
DELMARVA CHRISTIAN WRITERS' FELLOWSHIP

CHRISTMAS
Copyright © 2012 Candace F. Abbott

ISBN 978-1-886068-70-4
Christian Life • Religious and Inspirational
Personal Growth • Faith • Self-Help

Published by Fruitbearer Publishing, LLC
P. O. Box 777, Georgetown, DE 19947
302.856.6649 • FAX 302.856.7742
www.fruitbearer.com • info@fruitbearer.com

Cover illustration by Laura E. Pritchett
from a *Dear Ones* card inspired by Malorie Derby
Graphic Design by Candy Abbott
Edited by Wilma Caraway

Printed in the United States of America

Heath + Chelsea,
Hope you enjoy this
Christmas. Many
good articles - I have two
in here.
merry christmas!
Love mom - DeMon
12/12

CHRIS✝MAS

Dedicated

To Christian Writers
who faithfully handle the words
God entrusts to them.

Introduction

※

Established in 1993, Delmarva Christian Writers' Fellowship (DCWF) meets the third Saturday of every month in Tunnell Hall at the Georgetown Presbyterian Church, 203 North Bedford Street, Georgetown, Delaware, from 9 a.m. to 12:30 p.m. Meeting attendance runs from eight to twenty-eight. Many are new writers who are mentored by those who have been published. It is an informal gathering for critiquing and encouragement with resources to build up the Christian who writes. There is no membership fee, no formal agenda, and no pressure, but we do hold one another accountable to see progress in our writing. Meetings typically include a devotional, shared information, a teaching, manuscript critiques, and prayer. Friendships are fostered over lunch and between meetings. On occasion, we host day-long writing seminars or retreats and encourage participation in regional/national conferences.

This compilation of Christmas stories, devotionals, poems, and tidbits is our second publication. The first, *CHRIST IS NEAR: Advent Meditations* by Delmarva Christian Writers' Fellowship, was initially published in 2002 to give beginning writers an opportunity to see their work in print. Eight years later, it was completely revised, and the second edition was released in 2011.

Since then, many of our members have progressed in their writing, and two new groups have been formed: Vine & Vessels Christian Writers Fellowship (which meets the second Saturday of the month and hosts an annual conference), and Kingdom Writers Fellowship (which meets the second Tuesday evening of each month). Some of our members have relocated or passed away, and new members have joined our fellowship. The collection you hold in your hand is a small representation of the many writers who have been encouraged and who have encouraged others in their quest to write with excellence and delight, to the glory of God.

We hope you enjoy this family-friendly Christmas book. Who knows? Maybe it will spark a desire in you to write!

For more information, visit www.DelmarvaWriters.com, or call Candy Abbott, director, at 302.856.6649.

Table of Contents

CHRISTMAS

No Newborn Crib

Eva C. Maddox

No newborn crib lined with sterile sheet,
No nursery smelling soft and sweet,
No rocking chair, no diapers there,
The birthing room, stark and bare.

How could the Son of God appear
In such a place, so cold and drear?
I do not know, nor understand
Why this was part of the Savior's plan.

But this I know, and do believe
He came to die for you and me.
He left his home and came to earth
And doing so, gave us new birth!

A Manger Scene

Eva C. Maddox

He grew up before him like a tender shoot,
and like a root out of dry ground.
He had no beauty or majesty to attract us to him,
nothing in his appearance that we should desire him.

Isaiah 53:2 (NIV)

I have a manger scene that I carefully unwrap each December and arrange on top of our mantle. As a matter of fact, I have a large plaster of Paris manger scene that I placed outside on our lawn for years. However, it is so heavy I can no longer lift it. I have another small one that I sometimes place on the coffee table, and a miniature one inside a Christmas ornament. So many scenes depicting the birth of the Christ child!

I've noticed as the years pass that I see fewer manger scenes as I go about my Christmas shopping, but more beautiful trees decorated with twinkling lights and shiny ornaments. And who could miss jolly old Santa's "Ho, ho, ho?"

But one store actually had a rather large manger scene in their storefront window recently. I stopped and stared at it for a few minutes. The store had attempted to beautify the scene by giving the stable a roof of glittering white and tucking soft twinkling lights in the artificial blanket of snow surrounding it.

My spiritual eye took it all in. *How different the real scene must have been. The rough-hewn boards, strewn hay, and smelly animals were far from a place any woman would choose to give birth. Yet, in the crèche, a very young Mary sits serenely observing her child after having just experienced childbirth for the first time in a place where animals feed.*

I left there thinking that the true beauty of a manger scene can only be understood in the fullest sense by those who personally know Who that Babe in the manger represents.

Father, help me to remember Your birth this Christmas and rejoice in its significance.

Angel on Loockerman Street

Candy Abbott

The air was crisp and still on Loockerman Street in Dover that Thanksgiving Eve in 1972. Tender snowflakes began to fall as I carried my one-year-old daughter, all bundled up in her Christmas jacket, past storefronts decorated with twinkling white lights. As we strolled along, I marveled that we had the whole town to ourselves. It could have been magical if not for my recent meeting with the divorce attorney.

"Look," I said to Kim, pointing to a display in the jewelry store window. "Isn't that a pretty bracelet?" Determined not to let my emotional or financial situation color my daughter's world, I forced a lilt into my voice and gave her a playful squeeze. "You see, Hon? Window shopping can be just as much fun as buying things."

Oh, how alone I felt—not only there on the dimly lit sidewalk but in my life. I glanced up and around. Suddenly, a jolt of fear ran through me. We weren't alone after all! A man had rounded the corner at the end of the street and was walking straight toward us. There I was, a single mother with my baby in my arms. The man kept coming closer and closer. I tried to regain a sense of control as my eyes darted about seeking a quick escape route.

Then I glanced again at the gentleman who didn't really look all that threatening. In fact, he seemed downright pleasant.

He was a little man with a shiny black face—as black as the onyx bracelet I had been admiring moments before. He wore a top coat and tie, and it occurred to me that he may have just come from church. The moment his chocolate eyes connected with mine, his face lit up with the most genuine smile and the whitest teeth I'd ever seen. A pillow of white hair peeked out from beneath the brim of his wool hat.

Peace wrapped around my heart like a warm quilt. All apprehension vanished. I didn't know this stranger, but something about him made me feel like I was looking into the eyes of an old friend.

"Hello," I said when he got close enough for conversation. "The snow's a nice touch for Thanksgiving Eve, don't you think?"

"Yes, it is." He continued smiling, stopped in front of me, and held out something in is hand. "Here," he said. "This is for you."

I couldn't tell exactly what it was, but it looked like money, and I reacted instinctively. "Oh, no. I couldn't. But, thanks anyway."

"Please." He continued holding the money out to me, and I saw that it was a one dollar bill.

"No, really," I smiled. "That's very kind, but I can't take money from a stranger."

"But you must," he said, his smile never wavering. "The Lord told me to give this to you, and I must be obedient."

"Well," I chuckled. "In that case, I guess I'll just have to take it." The words were no sooner out of my mouth than his gift was in my hand.

I turned back to the jewelry store window and said to Kim, "Let's see now, what shall we buy with our new dollar?" And when I swiveled around to thank the man, he was gone.

That little guy sure moves fast!

I looked up and down the street wondering how he got away so quickly. There were no visible footprints on the sidewalk, which struck me as odd. It began to snow harder, so I decided we'd better be getting off the street ourselves.

That dollar stayed in my wallet for months, folded and tucked in a corner where I could look at it any time I needed assurance that I wasn't alone—that somebody cared. It wasn't the amount that mattered. It was the fact that the Lord cared enough to send a little black man out on a snowy, mystical night to encourage me just when I needed it most.

I parted with that dollar one Sunday in church when the usher passed the collection plate, and I realized it was all I had to give. It seemed like the right time to let it go, especially in light of that morning's sermon that reminded me of the stranger's kindness: "Do not forget to show hospitality to strangers, for by so doing some people have shown hospitality to angels without knowing it" (Hebrews 13:2, NIV). If he wasn't an angel, he certainly acted like one.

Fast forward to 2004 in Georgetown, Delaware. My second husband Drew and I had recently celebrated our 29th anniversary, and I was editing a manuscript for one of my publishing clients, Linda Ockles. Chapter three of her true story, *Perfect Heart,* took my breath away:

> I blacked out. My car was rolling, and I was yelling, screaming, and praying for God to help me. When my car finally stopped, it was upside down in the middle of a field. I released my seatbelt and fell to the roof.
>
> When I came to my senses, I looked outside the car and saw a little black man with white hair wearing a suit and tie. I wondered how in the world he could have been there so quickly after my car stopped flipping. How did he get there? He looked at me and smiled, and I noticed that he was a very tiny man. He said that he was there to help me.
>
> At the time, I was so happy to see someone that I didn't care if he was a stranger or not. I gave him my hands, and he helped me out of the car, pulling me out through the back window. Glass was shattered everywhere. The little man got me out without one cut or scratch. When he pulled me out, it felt like I was floating through the air.
>
> Then the man said, "Linda." *How did he know my name?* He told me to lie down and close my eyes and assured me again that he was there to help me. Then he stood and yelled to a house in the distance. He hollered and told the people to call 911. The man knelt back down to me, put his hands over my eyes, and told me I was going to be just fine.

A woman came, and the little man asked if she had a blanket to put under my head. I told her to call my family to let them know. She went to call my family and then came back. Again, the little man asked for a blanket. She said that she didn't think she had one. The man then asked if she was sure she didn't have an afghan in her trunk.

Then the woman remembered and said, "Oh, yes, I do have an afghan." She ran to her car to get it, returned, and put the afghan under my head. While this was happening, I heard the ambulance approaching.

Not long after the paramedics took over, the helicopter came. The police started asking a lot of questions. They asked me how I got out of the car. I looked around for the little man, but he wasn't there. I told the police that a little black man with white hair pulled me from the car. Everyone looked around, but he wasn't there.

Could God have sent an angel? It would be impossible for a real person to have been there that fast. But he was there in that field with me—a little black man with white hair wearing a suit and tie.

Reading this account in her manuscript gave me chills.

I know that man! He was the one who came to me on Loockerman Street, just when I needed encouragement the most.

How many other angels have I encountered but didn't recognize? How many angels have visited you?

*Every day
is a gift from God.
That's why it's called
the "present."*

Author Unknown

Eyes of Light

Betty Kasperski

The eye is the lamp of the body.
So, if your eye is healthy,
your whole body will be full of light;
but if your eye is unhealthy,
your whole body will be full of darkness.
If then the light in you is darkness, how great is the darkness!
Matthew 6:22-23 (NASB)

We all understand that our eyes are a precious part of our bodies. Our eyes are an efficient organ that allows us to see the morning sunlight, the smile from a loved one and even view the clock on the wall as we prepare the evening meal.

The eyes have also been called the window to the soul. Happy eyes register joy. Troubled eyes reveal pain. Angry eyes can threaten us.

Our Scripture suggests that healthy eyes are the light of the body. We see goodness in others and ourselves. Healthy eyes reflect a positive outlook, provide hope, and encourage others. But the big warning for us is that the unhealthy eye or insincere eye will plunge us into darkness. Not just a dark mood but a negative outlook on life that snuffs out our light.

If our light does not shine, it soon fails to exist. How can we share warmth or spread joy to others if we do not have it ourselves? We know how a gloomy day impacts our mood and that a power outage immediately interrupts our world. Let us be thankful for the gift of our eyes and remember we are to be *spiritual beacons* to others to share the light, His light.

∞

Gracious God, thank You for the light of day and the power of Your light in our lives. Let us remember to use our eyes to share your warmth and reflect your love, not only during this Christmas season but every day. In Jesus' name.

Cloaked with Good Intentions

Kris Penrod

She stood there staring at it—just a simple barn coat, unassumingly designed in a pleasing shade of brown. She reached for it, hanging there, and stroked the soft ripple of the corduroy collar. She knew he'd like it. She could picture him in it, protected from the cold as he worked away with a chainsaw in his hands clearing the land where they hoped to build a home someday.

It was Christmas. Although she had already picked up some gifts for him, somehow they didn't seem like enough. He was so good to her—he made her feel special, he protected her, and he had asked her to be his wife! She felt inadequate as she stared at the jacket, knowing that she could never afford to match the gifts he had already given her. But, if only she had one more gift—one more present to wrap, perhaps his "pile" would seem more worthy. Her Christmas funds were all but depleted, but in her mind, she justified the cost of giving him this jacket as she reached for the hanger. She lifted it from the rod where it had hung. It seemed heavy—a warm winter cloak, nice and weighty. Little did she know how much weight it would cause her to bear.

Before long, it was lying on the floor in her home. She stroked the fabric, smoothed the wrinkles, then lovingly folded it into a nice rectangle, swaddled it in tissue, and placed it with care in a box which she then wrapped in brightly colored paper. A bow and a card signed "with love" completed the package. The gift lay under the tree, awaiting the love and good intentions of the giver to be transformed into happiness and appreciation by her fiancé.

And, on Christmas Day, that's exactly what happened. But there was one catch—the jacket didn't fit. No problem. He liked the jacket and was quite content to wait until she could exchange it for one just like it that was the proper size. She mustered a smile, hoping he wouldn't detect the silent desperation in her voice as she said she'd return it. The other packages were opened, and happiness filled the air. Hugs and kisses and Christmas happiness permeated the room. She had never felt so happy or so loved. But there was an underlying worry in her gut, a little nagging piece of information that kept popping into her mind as the day went on. Through the travels and merriment of the festivities with friends and relatives, there was a tiny "pea" that continued to bother the princess.

Some time went by before the subject came up again and she told him, "I don't think I can return the jacket, I don't have the receipt." She tried to keep her voice from quivering and hoped he couldn't see her knees shaking. The gift she'd given with good intentions was not turning out as well as planned.

But she wasn't the only one who had ever given a jacket like this with good intentions only to find it not received with the joy the giver had in mind.

Several years before, a corduroy collared barn coat in a pleasing shade of brown hung in a store, examined by a loving grandmother who was considering the coat for her grandson. He was a strapping young fellow, still a teenager, but in her eyes, he would always be a little boy. And, of course, in his own eyes, he was already a man. She reached for the hanger and lifted it from the rod where it hung. It felt heavy.

It should be nice and warm.

She took it to the register and paid for it, feeling happy about her purchase. She had such good intentions. Surely, he would like to find it under the Christmas tree. She took it home and lovingly wrapped it in tissue and holiday paper. A bow and a card signed, "Love Granny," completed the package. The gift lay under the tree, awaiting the love and good intentions of the giver to be transformed into happiness and appreciation by the recipient.

On Christmas Day, that's not exactly what happened. The grandson opened the gift, but the jacket was not what he had expected. He mustered a smile and a "thank you," which said without words that he had already decided the jacket would never find its way onto his shoulders. The jacket was tossed aside with the other "not exactly what I wanted" gifts.

After the holidays, when the presents had to be picked up from around the tree and put away, the jacket so lovingly chosen by his grandmother ended up in a heap in the corner of his room. His grandmother never saw him wear it because he never did. But, she knew better than to ask about it.

Months later, the boy was clearing some things out of his room when his girlfriend saw the never-worn jacket and asked about it. He said he had gotten it from his grandmother but never liked it.

She asked what he was going to do with it, and he told her he was just going to throw it away.

"What a waste," she said and immediately thought of her stepdad as it seemed about his size. It was such a pleasing shade of brown, and it had such a soft corduroy collar. Besides, she had been taught all her life not to be wasteful. She knew there was no shame in making use of something that someone else had discarded. She picked up the jacket with good intentions and took it home with her.

She proudly handed it to her stepdad who received it with a smile and a heartfelt "thank you." The jacket had finally been received with the appreciation that it was first purchased to provide.

But, alas, the stepdad already had a variety of his own "favorite" jackets and, although he did appreciate the gift his stepdaughter had given to him, he just never seemed to find the proper occasion to wear the rugged barn coat. So, it hung in his closet for quite some time, waiting to be used for the purpose that it was created.

Jackets don't have feelings, I'm sure, but if they did, although proud to be as pristine as the day it was made, this one was longing to get out into the elements and the dirt and just keep someone warm. And that is exactly what would have happened to it—had it only been the correct size in the first place.

But now, on this Christmas, the fine jacket was the subject of anxiety for the young woman who had matured and grown during the years that the barn coat hung in her stepfather's closet. This jacket, woven with the fabric of good intentions, had now become fashioned by lies. Not the type of lies that would cause great pain for anyone, but lies, none the less.

The young woman was now at a turning point. Was she strong enough to tell the truth? Or would she somehow have to continue the masquerade and create yet another white lie to explain her inability to exchange the coat. She felt a knot in her stomach that wouldn't go away, but she knew what she must do.

So she did. The knot in her stomach moved to her throat and almost choked off the words as she stood in front of the man she loved. She opened her mouth but nothing came out at first. She swallowed hard, trying to hold back the tears. But, as the words came, so did the tears.

"I'm sorry, but I cannot return the coat. You see, I never bought it." *Although I fear that I may pay for it for a long time.*

The tears flowed faster and faster as she told the story behind the last-minute Christmas gift. Her words began to run like the tears and, between the "I'm sorrys" and the "I only wanted to get you one more things," she tried to interject as many "Can you ever forgive mes" as possible.

She couldn't look her fiancé in the eye as she told the story. Instead, as her confession spilled out, she looked down at the floor with embarrassment and shame. When she was through, there was silence. All she could do was to wait. She didn't dare look up.

The man was fighting with his own feelings, too. He was angry. He felt used and betrayed.

How could she even consider giving me something that originally belonged to someone else! How could she give me something that meant so little but at the same time meant so much? And, the "someone else"! Why, that first "someone else" had been so cruel to her in the past. That first "someone else" had been so callus and uncaring, so immature and ignorant. Why would I want to even consider putting this coat across my own shoulders?

He wanted to scream. He wanted to tear up the coat. He wanted to walk out the door. But, he couldn't. As a matter of fact, he couldn't even move. He was paralyzed by the crippling reality of the truth.

And, so was she. The truth . . . the truth . . . the same truth that had allowed her to finally feel free from the burden of deceit she had been carrying was causing him to feel the weight of the burden of anger. Moments passed, but they seemed like hours as the two of them stood in silence.

She sneaked a glance at him, but his eyes were closed. The expression on his face told her that his mind was racing, too. The waiting was agonizing. Was he working as hard as she to evaluate the past and reevaluate their chances for the future, trying to unravel the mystery of love? Or was he deciding how to tell her their engagement was off?

They both looked up at the same moment. Their eyes met.

At first, his eyes were angry. He stood there stiff and statue-like, holding her at bay with his gaze.

She could not speak. This was it. The man of her dreams was going to discard her like the miserable, unloved jacket.

Remorseful tears swelled larger in her eyes and ran down her flushed cheeks like a river. She squeezed her eyes closed and let the river flow, accompanied by soft, raggedy child-like sobs, as she waited for the dreaded words.

Instead, she felt his fingertips trace the tears on her cheeks, and her eyes sprung open to find the most loving expression she had ever seen on anyone's face.

"I had decided to tell you to leave," he said, stepping forward and enveloping her in his arms. "I'm such a jerk. How could I ever let you go?"

She sobbed harder, leaning into him, hoping she saw forgiveness in his eyes and letting the warmth of his embrace wash over her.

His words were soft—words she would remember the rest of her life. "The gift of the jacket is insignificant," he said. "The real gift you gave me is the gift of truth." He paused and lifted her chin.

"But I lied—time after time," she said.

He smiled. "And each little white lie was cloaked with good intentions. It must have taken every ounce of courage you could muster to tell me where the jacket really came from and why you couldn't return it."

Her tears began to subside.

"It's okay," he said. "Your intentions were pure. Everything you did, you did out of love. And you have proved your love for me by confessing." He took a deep breath. "And now it's my turn to set the tone for our future together. I give you the gift of trust." He held her eyes with his and said again, "It's okay."

Their wedding day came and went, and they celebrated many Christmases with an appreciation for one another that some couples never find.

Oh, and what became of the jacket? It's back on a hanger. But, this time it will bring great joy to the recipient. For you see, it now hangs in the local commission shop, where someone will happen across it and notice its pleasing shade of brown. He'll pull it out and stroke the ripples in the corduroy collar. He'll remove it from the rod it hangs on and realize that it's the right size. He will take it off the hanger and slip it on and let it fall onto his shoulders. Then he will look at the loved one who accompanied him to the shop and proclaim, "It's a perfect fit!" They won't have to pay much for it—nothing compared to the cost in the lives of those that it touched before. Once again, the simple cloak will prove that sometimes the greatest things in life are not expensive—they are priceless!

Drum Roll!

Betty Kasperski

After the Thanksgiving dishes are loaded into the dishwasher and a yummy piece of pumpkin pie has been consumed, we observe a special tradition in our family. It is time for the outside holiday lights to be lighted, officially kicking off the Christmas season.

As I gaze over the front lawn, I survey the soon-to-be illuminated objects: candy canes along the walkway; Santa and sleigh in position, with a family of reindeer leading the way; hundreds of lights inconspicuously tucked on the shrubs waiting to twinkle; handrails draped with red and green garland; and a snowman, complete with top hat, ready to go.

Guided by our "exterior illumination specialist" with his cords, prongs, and socket in hand, we assemble by the front curb for the start of the show. In chorus we chime, "Drum Roll," and make the sound—drrrrh, drrrrh, and the sparkle begins!

But wait, I forgot to mention the focus of the display, anchored right in the middle, glowing brighter than all the other items—the manger scene. There would be no celebration without the faith centerpiece—the birth of the Christ child. As we prepare our homes and our hearts for this holy season, let's remember the "Drum Roll" always begins with Him: The Light of the world!

Merry Christmas!

A Random Gift of Sweetness

David Michael Smith
As told by Dennis Malivuk

It was a dark and stormy night. Really, it was! But this isn't a spooky tale about a haunted house on Halloween evening, but rather one set in a petite Delaware town's local pharmacy the week before Christmas. And proof that God indeed does work in mysterious ways.

Tired, Dennis glanced at his watch and smiled. *Only forty-five more minutes until we close.* The store was nearly abandoned, despite the fact that Christmas was right around the calendar's corner. *Probably the rain.*

The automated doors opened, and a middle-aged couple entered with pace and purpose, wet from the precipitation. The man carried a portfolio under his trench coat as if precious cargo, certainly something of importance. Dennis offered his assistance.

"You print photos, right?" the man inquired with an accent that tipped Dennis off that the gentleman wasn't local. "We really need to get a few things done."

"Yes sir, machine's right over there," Dennis said, pointing past colorful, holiday displays featuring an assortment of gift ideas. "Let me assist you, please."

As the trio walked over to the kiosk that hosted the photographic equipment and supplies, labeled "Photo Center," Dennis noticed that the couple looked tired and sad. Dennis wondered, *Why is it the holidays, 'the most wonderful time of the year' as the song declares, brings with them such stress and melancholy?*

Dennis positioned himself behind the equipment to reacquaint himself with its functionality. "Okay, how can I help you good people?"

The man started to speak, but the words did not come. So his wife, grayish-blonde hair covered with a rain bonnet and wearing a stylish red raincoat, interceded.

"We have some photos from our wedding nearly 30 years ago we'd like to get copies of," she said. "Please make them pretty. They're for John's mother, my mother-in-law, Joyce."

Dennis smiled warmly at the couple. "That's very nice. A Christmas gift, huh?"

"Well, no. Not exactly. We've promised her these photos for years but always put it off. Maybe we were just lazy, or forgot, I don't know. She always wanted a set from our wedding day, but it just never happened. It's funny how things get away from you in life."

"Well, better late than never, right?" Dennis said.

John, the husband, nodded. The woman pursed her lips together tightly and gave a slight nod in agreement.

Quietly, Dennis went to work, but halfway through the process of reproducing a stack of about fifty photographs, the machine began to overheat. Somewhat embarrassed, Dennis called another employee, Sandy, to assist. It was nearly closing time, and Dennis did not want to fail this couple with their special gift quest. For nearly fifteen minutes the employees tinkered with the equipment, disassembled and then reassembled components, until finally, they returned to the task successfully. The couple never complained and patiently stood there throughout the ordeal, in dripping attire, politely participating in the typical light talk exchanged between store clerks and customers.

With only five photos left to copy, Dennis, with a note of excitement, exclaimed, "I just know your mom's going to be overjoyed to finally get these photos from you guys! I almost wish I could see her face when she opens them up."

There was a long, awkward pause from the couple. Dennis immediately sensed he had said something that initiated the discomfort.

"Sorry, I'm being a chatty Cathy tonight; we're almost done. Thank you for your patience, folks," Dennis said.

"No, you're fine, Dennis," John answered, reading the employee name tag. "You see, these photos are indeed for my mom. But she won't be able to see them. Unfortunately, you see, she died this week, and we're heading to the funeral scheduled for tomorrow afternoon. We'll put the photos in her casket, cradled in her arms . . ."

The man sighed heavily, and his wife wiped away a tear. "You were right, Dennis, 'better late than never,' huh?"

Dennis asked Sandy to finish the job, and he stepped away. The couple had been so patient, so kind, despite the equipment malfunctions and circumstances, all the while dealing with the personal pain of losing a loved one and right before Christmas. Dennis, in the season of giving, wanted to offer some token, some small gift, in exchange for their goodness and positive spirit. Without a clear sense of direction, he absently wandered down one of the aisles, randomly grabbed a seasonally decorated bag of red, green and gold foil-wrapped candied mints, and discreetly purchased them with his own cash. Then he bagged the item and pushed it aside.

The couple approached the register with their photos in hand for payment. Dennis smiled and rang up the purchase, thanked the couple again for their patience, and offered his condolences. They nodded and began to leave.

"Oh wait! Sorry, I nearly forgot," Dennis said. "It's nothing, really, but I wanted to get you two something for your incredible patience tonight with our stubborn equipment—and with it being so close to Christmas and all . . ." He handed them the plastic bag with the candy. The couple shyly accepted the gift and pulled out its contents. And immediately they both began to cry.

Dennis began to apologize.

"No, no, you're fine," the lady stammered with a smile. "You see, you just made our night, Dennis. The only way I can say it is you are an angel—our Christmas angel."

Dennis was dumbfounded. It was only a simple bag of chocolate mints.

The man explained, "You would never have known, but every Christmas when we visited my mother in New York for the holidays she gave us a gift card to our favorite restaurant chain, and something she would've quilted that year, and—" He couldn't finish the sentence.

"A bag of Andes chocolate mints," his wife concluded. Then she repeated, "A *Christmas* bag of Andes—the exact same thing you just gave us."

Dennis could not speak. Out of hundreds of items he could have selected from the shelves for this hurting couple, he had selected the one item that offered them hope, peace, joy, and love, the four traits of the Advent season announcing Christmas.

"Thank you, Dennis. We'll never forget you," John managed as they began to leave the store. "You have no idea how much this means to us!"

Then the couple departed into the rainy chill of night while Dennis silently locked up the store, turned off the lights, and set the alarm system. But not before purchasing a second bag of Andes chocolate mints, an early Christmas gift, to take home to his wife.

Movie Quote
Miracle on 34th Street (1947)

Fred Gailey:

"Faith is believing when common sense tells you not to. Don't you see? It's not just Kris [Kringle] that's on trial, it's everything he stands for. It's kindness and joy and love and all the other intangibles."

Suddenly!

Candy Abbott

"See, I will send my messenger, who will prepare the way before me.
Then suddenly the Lord you are seeking will come to his temple;
the messenger of the covenant, whom you desire, will come,"
says the LORD Almighty.
But who can endure the day of his coming?
Who can stand when he appears?
For he will be like a refiner's fire or a launderer's soap.

Malachi 3:1-2 (NIV)

"Suddenly!" What an exciting or unnerving word, depending on our relationship with the Lord. Those of us who walk with God in peace and uprightness, who eagerly await Christ's return, will rejoice in the promised suddenness of His appearing. But, for those who are breaking faith, "suddenly" can be a fearful thing. Who wants to come face-to-face with the Holy One who burns away our good intentions to expose selfish ambition, the Pure One who knows the sordid details of our secret sins and rebellious thoughts? Who can endure the day of His coming? Who can stand when He appears? Who?

We can—if we simply respond in faith to the LORD who has called us unto Himself; if we seek the guidance of the Holy Spirit; if we invite God to search our hearts and embrace His forgiveness when we stumble. If we delight in His Word and in His presence, we won't need to prepare for "suddenly," because it will be a joyous reunion with the One we already know, love, and trust.

Lord, we want our relationship with You to be so strong and secure that the suddenness of Your return will be as seamless as our next breath, our next heartbeat. Fill us with the joy of anticipation!

The Gift of Giving

Barry A. Jones

July 16 began a nightmare that turned into one of my biggest dreams come true.

Having arrived home from work, I piddled in the living room and bedroom, eventually making my way into the kitchen. Much to my surprise, I found the metal kitchen door had been pried up from the bottom corner, leaving a space open to the outdoors. It was obvious, even to my novice eyes, that the only thing that had prevented the culprit from entering had been the dead bolt that had been securely fastened.

Immediately, I called the police. While waiting for an officer to arrive, I called my friend, Toni. Knowing that she was a part of the women's prayer ministry that would be meeting that evening, I explained what had happened. I solicited prayer, giving her permission to share what had transpired with the other ladies. I know they covered me with prayer because at no time, then or since, have I been afraid.

On Thursday of the same week, July 19, I walked into my home, put down some bags on the kitchen counter, and proceeded to the bedroom. On the way, I tripped over something. Looking down, I discovered a round wooden object lying on the floor. *What in the world?* As soon as I opened the bedroom door, I realized the fan was missing and that someone had actually been in my home. I gathered my purse, keys, and cell phone, went out to my car, and called the police for the second time in one week. While waiting for them to arrive, I called Toni again, updated her on these new events, and asked that she pray with me.

Then, on July 30, two weeks after the first incident, my storage shed was broken into.

The day after the initial break-in, I received an e-mail from Kaye, who heads up our church's Compassionate Care ministry. She asked permission to have Bill, the coordinator of our S.O.S. program, come to my home to make sure my doors were secure and look into the possibility of installing a motion sensor security light. While S.O.S. is the universal signal for distress, at my church it stands for "Serving Our Savior." This wonderful group of people commit two Saturdays a month to doing light household tasks and repairs for singles and the elderly who can no longer do them.

Grateful for their offer, I consented to their assistance with gratitude. I knew that there was a lot of major work that needed to be done to my home. I also knew that I was in no position financially to have it done. I had taken care of all I could afford, up to that time, but so much more needed to be done. Though embarrassed to have someone else see my home in that condition, I decided not to let pride stand in the way of my safety.

Bill came to assess the situation and established a time to come back and do the work. Before he was scheduled to return, I received a call from Kaye who said Bill wasn't going to be able to make the appointment. Instead, Larry would come, as they wanted to get the work taken care of as soon as possible. I agreed to the change.

When Larry came, he determined that the door frame wasn't sturdy enough to be adequately secured. He also could not locate an electrical feed to my storage shed that previously had a security light affixed to it.

Armed with this new information, it was time to make some tough choices. Should I continue "as is," trusting God to provide the funds needed to make necessary repairs as He saw fit? Or should I revisit the thought of getting rid of my home and moving into income based housing or renting a room somewhere? These were avenues that I had explored in the past.

I received a phone call from our assistant pastor. "Barry," he said, "we've made a decision to repair your home." I was both elated and humbled by his words. After all, I knew the magnitude of what needed to transpire. In Scripture, we are admonished not to forsake the assembling of ourselves with like-minded believers and to do good to all men as we have opportunity, especially unto them who are of the household of faith (Hebrews 10:25). Recently, my pastor shared that the decision was made based on my church family's ability to see the Light of Christ in my life and the relationship we share as a family of believers. They "knew" me.

At the beginning of the year, the Lord told me that He was "making all things new." He certainly has been true to His Word in providing me with a "new" home. Bill and the S.O.S. team came to my rescue, doing "major" repairs. To date I have been blessed with new doors, floors, floor covering, a new deck, furniture, and exterior painting. I was even given a new exterior light that enhances the beautiful paint job. Soon to come are interior painting and/or papering, and new tables and lamps to go with the new furniture and window treatments.

One of my prayers, as I asked God to provide a way for me to be able to take care of what needed to be done in my home, was that He would do it in such a way that the world would know it was Him and Him alone. He answered that prayer by allowing my neighbors (who are unchurched) to rally around me after the break-ins. He then allowed them to see the evidence of His love for me through the sacrificial ministry of my church family.

I am grateful to God for all of the material things that He has blessed me with. They have made my home so much more inviting. I am even more deeply grateful for the tremendous outpouring of love with which everything has been done. The love is so strong, it's almost palpable.

My church is truly "a first-century church in the twenty-first century." In the words of our assistant pastor, "I'm glad that we have a church family with both the heart and the finances to do something like this."

As I think about the precious gift that I've been given, I think of our heavenly Father's much more precious gift to all of mankind. Wrapped in flesh and sent to earth that first Christmas morning in the form of a newborn baby, the Son of God became the Son of Man so we could be reconciled back to the Father.

Now there is a choice each of us must make. Like me, we must make an individual decision about what to do with the gift that we have been given by Him. Will we accept it and allow it to bless and enhance our lives? Or will we allow pride and self-will to rob us of a quality of life that was prepared for us before the foundation of the world?

The gift of giving has the ability to last throughout eternity. It's all about one Person. In our pastor's words, "His name is JESUS!"

Nativity Chant

Faye Green

Through blackness searching, searching
To the place of birthing.
Timeless dream perching, perching
For the end of waiting.

From the light guiding, guiding
To the innocents abiding.
Heaven to earth colliding, confiding
Dawn of a new dating.

Seek the infant sleeping, sleeping
See the mother weeping.
Man the answer seeking, seeking
The Word is believing.

Find the calm blessing, blessing
From the past so pressing.
Deity dressing, caressing
The Word is living.

The Ring

Malorie Drake Derby

There are two gold rings on my left hand. One is a ring of covenant, and the other is a ring of redemption. The first was placed there on the day I married Brian. The second, he gave to me on Valentine's Day, the second year of our marriage.

Three weeks after our marriage, my husband was shipped to South Korea to serve for thirteen months. On his return, we relocated to Selfridge Air Force Base in Michigan. It was just us, living in base housing, with one twin bed and our usual fare of tomato soup and grilled cheese sandwiches for dinner. Money was tight, and every cent had to be carefully spent. During that time, we began our lifelong love of meandering through flea markets. It was an inexpensive date and a free continuing education course in the value and history of one man's junk and another man's treasure.

That year, we celebrated Valentine's Day by visiting a new flea market. As we strolled through the cluttered aisles of possibilities, Brian stopped to pick up a 14-karat gold ring that matched his wedding band. After haggling with the vendor, he bought it for me for two dollars, placed it on my finger, and said, "I will love you forever."

Fourteen years passed, and neither of the two bands was ever taken off my finger, until—one Sunday at our church. The pastor asked for funds to build a new school, something very dear to my heart. But again, money was tight, and there was no extra to give. I got out of my seat, went forward, and presented my Valentine's Day ring.

"Sell the ring," I said. "And whatever you get for it, please put in toward the new school."

I returned to my seat. Brian never said a word.

Christmas Eve of that year was filled with present-wrapping, trying to keep two young ones somewhat sedate, and preparations for our annual family dinner. In the midst all of this, Brian put his arms around me and kissed me while handing me a small blue velvet box with a golden ribbon tied into a bow.

"Open it," he said.

With floured hands, I gently pulled the ribbon and slowly opened the velvet box. I gasped. Inside was my Valentine's Day ring! The tears in my eyes asked the questions, *How? Why?*

Brian explained that, before leaving church that day, he went to the pastor and said, "Whatever it costs, I want to redeem the ring."

My two-dollar ring was redeemed for $80.

He placed it on my finger and said, "I will love you forever."

My Broken Angel

Barbara Creath Foster

Every year, I make my own Christmas cards, with original art and a poem.

My all-time favorite card is one I call *My Broken Angel*. When I created her, I tilted her halo and gave her more troubles. Somehow, her wing got bent, and the string on her harp broke. Why? Because nobody's perfect. We all have problems of some sort.

Poor Little Angel!
Life's not going well
With broken wings
And broken things.
Her halo's tilted.
Her dreams seem wilted.
She has, to her dismay,
One more bad-hair day.
She sings as she goes,
In spite of her woes.

Bright Little Angel!
Her task is to tell
About Jesus' birth
Bringing Peace to Earth
With Good Will to Men.
Reminding us when
Joy seems to have flown,
And our troubles have grown,
To cast every care
On our God in Prayer.

*And we know that in all things
God works for the good of those who love him,
who have been called according to his purpose.
Romans 8:28 (NIV)*

While making this card in 2004, I had a routine doctor's visit and a fleeting thought as I was about to leave home. *Why not take my angel to give to my doctor?* When he rushed into the exam room, looking very harassed, I gave him the card. He read it, looked at me with a smile and said, "Thank you. I needed this." Several other people later remarked about how true the card is—that we need to remember to take our problems to our God in prayer.

My prayer is that my Broken Angel blesses you today.

∞

This is a partial reprint from Barbara's article "Celebrating Christmas: Favorite Barb's Cards" published in her son John's online newsletter, *Sense and Non-Sense*, November 27, 2011.

Love
is what's in the room
with you at Christmas
if you stop opening presents
and listen.

❦

Author Unknown
(attributed to a 7-year-old named Bobby)

Collaring the Strays

Claire Smith

The violence, having shattered the joy of Christmas Eve, had passed, leaving destruction in its wake. Quiet descended upon the ruin, a quiet utterly devoid of peace. The house was in shambles. A toppled tree, broken lights, shattered ornaments, and dislodged decorations lay strewn about in bright mockery of the season of love and kindness.

Arabella Karlin, nicknamed Bel, lay on the living room sofa, finally asleep. She had cried herself into exhaustion, less distraught at the loss of her painting than at the betrayal of her father who had stolen it. The injury was severe. Even deeply asleep, Bel still cried, her breath expelled in soft shuddering sobs. I gently covered her with an afghan.

Evelyn, Bel's mother, rocked in a chair by the fireplace, huddled in upon herself, a shawl clutched around her thin frame. A bruise darkened the left side of her forehead. The firelight glistened on her cheeks, wet with unchecked tears.

I kept an unasked vigil. I couldn't leave. Neither could I sit still. I walked about gathering the decorations and restoring them to their previous places. I lifted the tree upright, found a broom, and began to sweep up the broken glass. The pieces made a tiny tinkling sound in the silence. My mind numb with shock, I worked diligently as if tidying up the edges of disaster could reestablish reason and order.

Not knowing what to do with the collapsed easel, I set it up again in the small alcove just off the living room. There it stood, as forlorn as a mother bereft of her child. The treasure it had so recently and proudly held had been wrenched away, vanishing into the dark night, its fate unknown.

As I looked at the easel, I could see the painting as clearly in my mind as if it still graced the wooden stand. Bel had painted a rugged landscape, a scene that could have fit into the highlands of Scotland or the foothills of the Rockies with equal ease. To the left was a sheepfold. A vigilant border collie guarded the entrance, keeping a responsible eye on both the sheep in the pen and its master. In the background, two other dogs herded strays toward the fold. On the right, Bel had painted a treacherous terrain. In the foreground, a sheep, already in trouble, had its nose pointed for more. The central figure, a shepherd, stretched his hand toward the wayward sheep, his fingers almost touching it. He could have easily reached it had he not been struggling with another sheep obviously trying to help and just as obviously in the way. The expressions Bel had given the sheep and the shepherd were studies in themselves. She called her painting *Collaring the Strays.*

Gifted with rare talent, Arabella Karlin had painted a masterpiece. Suddenly the pain caught up with me as realization sank in. Bel's masterpiece was gone, perhaps forever, and much of the fault was mine.

It was a scheme I had invented a long time ago to deal with folks who needed help, but who were too proud or too stubborn to take it. When I knew of a need, I called or visited the person involved and asked if my drama group and I could borrow their house or yard or garage or whatever, for some location practice. Then I would gather my drama group, give them the briefest of plot sketches, and off we would go. As a thank you, we would leave the props consisting of the goods or services needed. The kids gained some excellent experience and, at the same time, met a need. Up until now, it had been foolproof.

My daughter alerted me to Bel's situation. The family couldn't afford to show their daughter's painting. Could I fix things? Fully confident, I trotted out my scheme and went to pay a call on Evelyn Karlin. I met severe opposition right from the start. Nothing I said could shake her.

"I don't understand why you are so persistent. I appreciate your concern, but why should you care so much?" Evelyn asked on my seventh visit.

"I've seen Bel's painting. She should be encouraged. She isn't just talented, she's highly gifted."

"That's true, but, believe me, now is not the time. It isn't just the money, although that's problem enough as you can see." She waved a hand to indicate her neat but meager kitchen where we were having tea. "Maybe when she gets to college and finds the right people. Talent praised too much, too soon, can cause problems. I know you don't understand . . ."

"Is it her father who disapproves?" I asked carefully. I knew very little about Bel's father, only what my kids had told me—that he was a blue collar worker who found it hard to hold a steady job.

"Well, yes and no . . . I love my daughter very much, but there are others to consider. I desperately want to keep history from repeating itself. I . . . Can you keep a secret?" she asked abruptly.

"I've been known to," I replied with some amusement.

"I mean seriously." She replied so earnestly that I sobered immediately.

"I have something to show you, but the information *must not* leave this house. Will you promise me?"

"I give you my word."

"Then come with me. Maybe then you will understand."

Evelyn led me up to the third floor of the old rambling turn-of-the-century house. We walked to the end of the hall. Taking a key from the pocket of her sweater, she unlocked a door, pushed it open, and stood back to allow me to enter first. I stopped short and stared.

The studio filled one whole end of the house and contained dozens of paintings, some hanging on the walls, some stacked together on the floor. Near the center of the large room, where a cluster of windows let in the north light, stood an easel bearing an unfinished canvas.

I walked to the nearest framed painting to inspect it more closely. I peered closer yet to read the signature, and I was shocked again. Understanding dawned. Awed, I turned to Evelyn.

"Victor Karlin! Your husband—Bel's father—is *the* Victor Karlin?"

Evelyn nodded.

"No wonder Bel is so good." I murmured as I turned and walked to the easel. Even only half finished, I could easily see the Karlin trademark, bright colors and a reality that gave the impression that the subject could at any moment turn and speak from the canvas. I put out a tentative hand and touched the paint on the palette sitting atop a tall stool standing to one side of the easel.

"This is fresh paint! Is he . . . Is he painting again?"

"A little. He never really stopped. Victor seems to be compelled to paint."

"After all these years . . . He's lost none of his talent."

"I hope and pray that it's the beginning of a complete return."

"I thought he had destroyed all his paintings."

"That's the way the story goes. But, as you can see, it's not true."

"What the critics wouldn't do to discover a cache like this. They'd go nuts!"

"That's the thing that must *never* happen! I truly don't know what Victor would do if someone showed his pictures before he was ready. I wouldn't want to find out."

"What happened?" I asked. Evelyn safely locked the door, pocketed the key, and we returned to the kitchen.

"I don't know the full story. Victor won't talk about it.

Something hurt him badly. Victor started out needing to put color and forms on canvas. He had a friend once, a critic who made promises of wealth and fame. It divided Victor's attention. Then someone pulled the rug out, and Victor crash-landed head first into reality. I think Victor felt betrayed by the world, by God, and most of all, by his friend. He turned to alcohol. It caught him, and he hasn't been free since. He sold almost everything of value in the house. Then, six months ago he started treatment, just like that. I keep praying."

"And the children? Do they know?"

"They know he's an alcoholic, but I don't think they connect their dad with the famous Victor Karlin. They've never seen him paint. He cleared everything away from view when Brad was two, and Bel was only six months. Victor was going to let them know when he presented Bel with her sixteenth birthday gift, that half-finished painting you saw. I hoped that he would finish it on time, more for himself than for Bel. I hoped that there was a light at the end of the tunnel, but . . . . Now I don't know what to do for Bel's birthday."

"What if we simulate a showing? Nothing official, just a party of kids dressed up to act like critics and painters and connoisseurs and the general public. Could be fun."

"Do you ever give up on anything? Where could we have it?"

"Here. That way we can keep things in control."

"Keep control." My words came back to mock me. What irony. Was anything ever *less* in control?

I had arrived early this morning, and we had worked steadily cleaning and decorating. We had planned the "showing" for early afternoon so the house would be empty of guests before Victor arrived home at six. By the time we had finished the preparations, Evelyn's eyes were shining. She had been away from parties for a very long time.

Around noon, the two of us went to my house so I could change and Evelyn could try on a lovely dress I had never been able to wear. We were gone less than an hour. We arrived back to a situation fused and primed like a powder keg.

I haven't a clue which child discovered the upstairs studio or the key to the locked door. I have no idea who had decided to bring Victor Karlin's paintings out of hiding. Had gallery pros planned it, they couldn't have found a more fitting compliment to introduce Bel into the world of recognized artists than for her masterpiece to be surrounded by her father's canvases.

I have absolutely no idea how Bill Parker, our local high school art teacher, found out about the "showing" or how he managed to contact real live critics and connoisseurs on Christmas Eve Day, but there they were. As I had predicted, they were ecstatic about the Karlin paintings. They immediately surrounded Evelyn, inundating her with questions. Then the spark arrived, and the powder keg blew!

Victor Karlin, home early, entered the room full of people. Silence spread like a ripple across the room. The last to feel the effect was a critic from a large gallery in a nearby city. Everyone could clearly hear his voice as he spoke to Bel.

"Young lady, you are every inch as gifted as your father. I'm sure I could arrange a showing for you. There's money to be made from talent like yours."

"NO!" Karlin's bellow of rage shocked everyone into immobility. The volcano inside him erupted. Like a tornado, he whipped around the room, wreaking havoc. His eyes found his wife, and he spat out venomously, "You traitor!"

"No, Victor, I didn't . . ."

"I told you not to encourage her!" he shouted at his wife. Spinning around, he pinned his daughter with hate-filled eyes. "This is all your fault! Well, I'm putting an end to this right now! Forever!"

From some pocket, a wicked looking knife leapt into his hand, its blade sharp and deadly. Holding it by the haft, he raised his arm and lunged at Bel's painting.

"No!" Evelyn intercepted her husband, standing protectively before the painting. With a strength that surprised me, she swung her arm and connected with her husband's wrist. Stunned more by surprise than by her strength, Karlin dropped the knife.

"Get out of my way!" he growled menacingly.

"No! I've stood by and watched you ruin your own life. I will not permit you to wreck our daughter's life, as well. One tragedy in this family is more than enough!"

"Oh, is it?" he asked through clenched teeth. "We'll see about that!" Karlin swung his arm with the force of wrath behind it, caught his wife on the left temple, and felled her like a rag doll. Then he snatched the painting and vanished into the night.

"Oh, Lord," I wept silently. "If only I had asked You first, none of this would have happened. I'm so sorry I got in Your way. Do my lessons always have to cause someone pain?" I wept silently. "On this night when we celebrate the great miracle of Your birth, will You perform another? Will You touch Victor's heart and unite him with his family? Please, Lord, bring him home."

In the small, chilly hours of Christmas morning, the soft sound of a door opening awakened me. From my chair in a dark corner, I saw Victor Karlin cross the living room and restore his daughter's painting to the easel. I saw him touch it with gentle, respectful, loving hands. I saw him bend down over his sleeping daughter and kiss her forehead, heard the murmured, "I'm so sorry, Bel. Forgive me." I saw him go to his wife, kneel before her, and gather her into his arms.

Covered by the sound of their mingled weeping, I shrugged into my coat and slipped out, started my car, and headed for home.

Christmas Blessings

May your life be
Filled with joy—
Not in beautiful
Gift or toy—
But wrapped in the glorious, awesome love
Of Jesus Christ and God above!

Verse and photo by
Kristin Caraway Whitaker

Shepherds

Michele Jones

When the angels had gone away from them into heaven
the shepherds began saying to one another,
"let us go straight to Bethlehem then and see this thing
that has happened which the Lord has made known to us."
So they came in a hurry and found their way to Mary and Joseph,
and the baby as He lay in the manger.

Luke 2:15-16 (NASB)

Imagine you are one of those shepherds out in the fields on a dark, silent night. There you are, minding your own business, when the night sky is filled with the glory of the Lord that seems to shine from every corner of the universe, but is emanating from one supernatural being. You are absolutely terrified and fall to the ground. The angel comforts you, saying "Fear not," and then proceeds to explain the magnificent news about Christ's birth and where you can find Him. You are barely able to grasp the magnitude of what you are hearing when, suddenly, the whole area is filled with a great company of heavenly beings praising and glorifying God!

You and your fellow shepherds leave everything behind to go in search of the Messiah. Your flocks are your livelihood, and leaving them behind is a great risk. The sheep could easily wander away. They could become prey to some wild animal. Yet you and the other shepherds make the sacrifice to go and find the Christ child.

Scripture says the shepherds hurried.

They left it all behind and purposely sought out the Savior.

Are we willing to make the sacrifice to go and find Him? Are we willing to leave our past behind and find Christ who can forgive us and restore us to be all that we can be for the kingdom? Jesus' birth is part of a greater plan to bring us back to the right relationship with our heavenly Father. Sin divided us from Him. Christ came to break that division and bring restoration.

Christ is waiting, my friend. Hurry!

Lord, we pray that You would make us like the shepherds, available to You and eager to seek You out. Give us the strength and boldness to leave the cares of this world behind and follow You.

Light

Gail Atlas

"The people walking in darkness have seen a great light;
on those living in the land of deep darkness a light has dawned."
Isaiah 9:2 (NIV)

The shopping trip had been unsuccessful, not yielding the Christmas presents I had hoped to find. My husband and I were tired and hungry. It was late, and we were far from home. The road was dark, the weather drizzly and dreary—cold, but not cold enough to snow.

"I think I see a light," I said, breaking the silence. "There's a shopping center up on the left, probably with a place to eat."

Bright, welcoming rays of light streamed from the restaurant, beckoning us in. As I pulled my coat around me and headed toward the light, I thought, *It's Christmas, when we celebrate Jesus as the Light of the world.* And right then, light was a very wonderful thing.

That night, the light of the restaurant represented direction. We needed food, and the light pointed the way to a place to eat. It gave us illumination. We could see by the light that the restaurant was open and offered the kind of food we liked to eat. By following the light, our current needs could be filled. The light of the restaurant served as a warning, as well. Because of it, I avoided a large, cold puddle. The light also meant warmth. I couldn't wait to get inside as I shivered across the few feet of parking lot.

That night my needs were trivial compared to the eternal needs that separate us from God, the reason Jesus came to be our Light. His direction, His revelation and fulfillment of our need, His warning of sin, and His protection are major gifts, not to be overlooked. We live in a world just as sin-darkened as it was more than 2,000 years ago, and we so much need His Light on a grand scale. I am eternally grateful that His Christmas Light has brought me guidance, clarification, caution, and shelter. And I am also grateful for that one night when a welcomed light caused me to contemplate what the greater Light can mean.

Lord, thank You for being our Light. Thank You for allowing us to celebrate Your coming each year. And thank You for all the things You teach us about Yourself. Continue to teach us who You are through the simple things we see all around us.

A Tree for Remembering

Jean Davis

Last year, oranges were $1.00 each. *My dad would never have believed it!* I remembered how thrifty he was and how much oranges meant to him, especially at Christmas. When he was a child, he looked forward to receiving a single apple or orange as his Christmas gift each year.

One day in mid-December when I entered our local grocery store and saw a hand-written sign above a display of bagged oranges—"Navel Oranges, 8 pounds, $4.99"—I was pleased with my good fortune. I got them home, opened the bag, and poured all 13 oranges into a large blue bowl. What a great bargain!

My husband Vergil, the practical one, dampened my enthusiasm when he came in from work and looked at the overflow. "Jean," he said, "how will we use all these oranges before they ruin?"

We ate oranges for breakfast and oranges for snacks. I added orange segments to spinach salad. I offered some oranges to our daughter, but she only took a few since she had recently bought her own bag.

Was it happenstance that I ran across an article that gave instructions about using fruit for Christmas decorations?

Cut an orange crosswise into slices a quarter-inch thick, bake the slices in a 225-degree oven for two to three hours on a cookie sheet lined with foil or parchment until the slices dry out, thread each slice with ribbon and hang as an ornament.

I can do that! So on the day I added lights to our bare Christmas tree, I sliced oranges to bake. As the fragrant aroma of citrus filled the kitchen, I thought about my dad and his childhood and about my growing up years. I loved him so much!

As I threaded the orange slices with ribbon, a story my friend, Carolyn, told me came to mind. One of ten children, every year for Christmas, she got an orange in one of her own socks she'd hung on the mantel. That was it.

Then my thoughts traveled halfway around the world to an orphanage in the Ukraine. I was touched by a photograph I had received from my friend, Theresa, while on her mission trip there. Each child held a Christmas box, and on top of each box was an orange or a banana. "They don't get fruit often," she said in her letter. "Fruit is such a treat for them."

As I hung my new ornaments on the tree, I prayed for the orphans.

The light shimmering through the baked orange slices made them look like stained glass. My heart was already full when

Vergil came in and saw the new ornaments on our tree along with a single wooden cross and a single wooden star.

"Oh, Jean!" he said. "This is our best tree yet. It's beautiful."

Over the years, I've lost my excitement for many things Christmas. Perhaps I've been jaded by Christmas displays in stores in October, the abundance of non-essential stuff, the invitation to credit card debt, and the lack of simplicity. But this year . . . this year, I can hardly wait for one of our local grocery stores to put oranges on sale in December. I'll slice two or three crosswise, bake at 225 degrees, and thread with ribbon. Finally, I've found something that, for me, breaks the stronghold of commercialism. I'll tie the orange slices on the branches of our tree, and with a heart filled with gratitude and love, I will remember the importance of simplicity and the things that really matter.

*Never worry about
the size of your Christmas tree.
In the eyes of children,
they are all 30 feet tall.*

❦

Larry Wilde
The Merry Book of Christmas

Blue Christmas?

Judi Folmsbee

"Heaven and earth will pass away,
but my words will never pass away."
Matthew 24:35 (NIV)

It was Christmas 2009, and I was without my husband, Rick. He died suddenly of a heart attack in June. We had shared thirty-eight Christmases together. Going to church was the hardest thing for me to do. How was I supposed to feel the joy everyone else was feeling? I just didn't have it. I had no excitement for the holiday. Rick was always Mr. Christmas. He enjoyed the holiday—from the manger scene and church services to the cookies, gifts, and especially family time. This year was painfully different.

Every year, we attended the late Christmas Eve service. This year, I attended church in Virginia with relatives. It was a beautiful church. The first thing I laid my eyes on was a handcrafted cradle with baby Jesus lying inside. Before the service started, we listened as familiar Christmas carols were played. Christmas ties, sweaters with Christmas scenes, velvet, ribbons, and even fur were the norm for the day.

The church was decorated with beautiful greenery and vibrant red berries. The smell of fresh boughs of pine and holly reminded me of times when Rick and I would take walks in the woods in search of just the right branches to decorate our home. When I read that poinsettias were given in Rick's name, the tears I was trying to hold back fell from my eyes like melting icicles.

It was a great holiday service, but I was just going through the motions. It was a befitting way to honor the birth of Jesus, but my heart just wasn't in it. The knot in my stomach just wouldn't allow excitement or joy.

Close to the end of the service, handheld unlit candles were distributed to everyone in the congregation. Each candle had a paper protector around the middle like a skirt. As I received my candle, I grabbed it firmly in my hand. This was a solemn part of the service. As I waited for my candle to be lit, all of a sudden the candle flew out of my hand, as if someone had bumped my elbow. It sailed through the air and landed in the pew in front of us. My family and I had no choice but to give a hearty belly laugh. I am sure we disturbed others around us during this quiet time. Fortunately, it did not hit anyone, and it wasn't lit.

After the candle incident, I felt sure God had sent an angel to hit my arm. Rick believed in laughter and great family time.

Rick was letting me know that he knew it wasn't the same, but laughter helps when you hurt.

I was reminded that night that life is for the living. We will never forget our loved ones. It was a wakeup call for me to live, laugh, and love . . . again.

O Lord, thank You for giving us loved ones to share our lives. Help us realize that life is too short, and we must live each day for You. Thank You for allowing us to laugh during tough times, while always being connected to You.

Christ's Bell

THE BELL
I KNOW WHO I AM
I am God's child (John 1:12).
I am Christ's friend (John 15:15).
I am united with the Lord (1 Cor. 6:17).
I am bought with a price (1 Cor. 6:19-20).
I am a saint (set apart for God) (Eph. 1:1).
I am a personal witness of Christ (Acts 1:8).
I am the salt & light of the earth (Matt. 5:13-14).
I am a member of the body of Christ (1 Cor. 12:27).
I am free forever from condemnation (Rom. 8:1-2).
I am a citizen of Heaven. I am significant (Phil. 3:20).
I am free from any charge against me (Rom. 8:31-34).
I am a minister of reconciliation for God (2 Cor. 5:17-21).
I have access to God through the Holy Spirit (Eph. 2:18).
I am seated with Christ in the heavenly realms (Eph. 2:6).
I cannot be separated from the love of God (Rom. 8:35-29).
I am established, anointed, sealed by God (2 Cor. 1:21-22).
I am assured all things work together for good (Rom. 8:28).
I have been chosen and appointed to bear fruit. (John 15:16).
I may approach God with freedom and confidence (Eph. 3:12).
I can do all things through Christ who strengthens me (Phil. 4:13).
I am the branch of the true vine, a channel of His life (John 15:16).
I am God's temple (1 Cor. 3:16). I am complete in Christ (Col. 2:10).
I am hidden with Christ in God (Col. 3:3). I have been justified (Romans 5:1).
I am God's co-worker (1 Cor. 3:9; 2 Cor 6:1). I am God's workmanship (Eph. 2:10).
I am confident that the good works God has begun in me will be perfected (Phil. 1:5).
I have been redeemed and forgiven (Col. 1:14). I have been adopted as God's child (Eph. 1:5).
I belong to God.
Do you know
who you are?

Author Unknown

Submitted by Wilma Shepard Caraway

Light of Revelation

Lori Ciccanti

Sovereign Lord, as you have promised,
you now dismiss your servant in peace.
For my eyes have seen your salvation,
which you have prepared in the sight of all people,
a light for revelation to the Gentiles
and for glory to your people Israel.
Luke 2:29-32 (NIV)

During the holiday season, I especially enjoy sending old-fashioned greeting cards to family and friends as an expression of my faith. Since I am very selective about my choice in cards, I carefully take the opportunity to remind others about the true meaning of Christmas.

One year, I was blessed to find a beautiful Christmas card designed by the "Friends of Israel" ministry. An excellent representation of the gospel message was depicted by the old prophet Simeon, whom the Lord revealed would not die until he saw the Messiah of Israel. The Scripture above is one of my favorites for two reasons.

CHRISTMAS

First, it clearly identifies salvation as a person, not an act.

Second, the same magnificent light which was revealed to Simeon had a purpose for both the Gentile nations and Israel: for the one, it was revelation; for the other, glory.

Another of my favorite Scriptures is John 17:3 (NIV) because it reveals the true meaning of eternal life, "Now this is eternal life: that they may know you, the only true God, and Jesus Christ, whom you have sent." Clearly, this life does not simply exist after death, but involves the intimate knowledge of the true God while we yet live.

Therefore, connecting both Scripture passages, eternal life begins with knowledge of the true God, and that knowledge results in the experience of salvation through the Person of His Son.

Salvation and eternal life are the priceless gifts that God has given to those who believe. According to the Scriptures, we cannot have one without the other. Psalm 36:9 (NIV) states, For with you is the fountain of life; in your light we see light. Thus, at the very moment of faith, His light of revelation touches the eyes of our heart, allowing the actual life of God to dwell in us.

Lord, we praise You for the people walking in darkness who have seen this great light of revelation in the face of Your Son, Jesus Christ. We thank You that through Him, we have the assurance of eternal life. Now, Lord, let Your servants rise and shine, for Your glory has risen upon us. Permit us to proclaim Your peace to those living in the shadow of death. And all God's people will say, "Amen!"

In the Fullness of Time

Eddy Jones

"But when the fullness of time came,
God sent forth His Son,
born of a woman,
born under the Law,
so that He might redeem those who are under the Law,
that we might receive the adoption as sons."
Galatians 4:4-5 (NASB)

IN THE FULLNESS OF TIME . . . What does that mean?
　　That I should care such knowledge to glean?

Time passes and evaporates before our very eyes,
　　So how can it be full, is one of my whys?

In the fullness of time, God sent His Son.
　　What's the big deal for such a focus on One?

Born of a woman like that of no other—
　　A young maiden, a virgin, and devoted mother.

Born of a woman and under the Law,
    The Law that showed sin and was given to all.

The Law showed us sin but it could not heal.
    Sinners are doomed as if from God they could steal.

Why was He sent at the time that He came?
    Why not sooner or later—isn't it all the same?

Why in the world did He come when He did?
    Was the timing so important for our sins to make a bid?

The context of time, however, shows a unique convergence,
    As time before and after His coming just didn't make sense.

For centuries, men and nations have waged evil and war,
    But God's Son came to open a much-needed door.

So enters a new scene which the world's never seen,
    A time of peace for the nations—that's what I mean.

From the time of Caesar Augustus is when it all began . . .
    The Pax Romana and peace for man.

For 200 years, peace entered the land.
    It was then that we saw the emergence of the God-man.

At the time men watched their flocks by night
    God sent the Good Shepherd.

When evil reigned in Jerusalem
    God sent the King of Kings.

After hundreds of years of prophecies
  God sent the Redeemer to fulfill them.

During a rare time when the world was calm,
  God sent the Prince of Peace.

IN THE FULLNESS OF TIME . . . What does that mean?
  God sent His Son for our sins to wash clean.

What the angels sang to the shepherds that night is still true today,
  Great tidings of peace and joy can still help you find the way.

Time fully came for His first appearance,
  Time to seek and save and help us find repentance.

But there is yet to be another time which has yet to fully come,
  When Christ shall return and gather only some.

So when we look back through the corridors of time,
  Let us remember His coming.

We remember how He came . . . fully human.
We remember His life . . . fully perfect.
We remember His sacrifice . . . the price fully paid.

IN THE FULLNESS OF TIME, He is coming again,
  For those who believe and in His eyes have no sin.

So what time is it, you may wonder as another season goes by?
  Time for you to remember the gift of grace and again
  wonder why?

Yes, this can all be IN THE FULLNESS OF TIME.

Christmas gift suggestions:

To your enemy, forgiveness.
To an opponent, tolerance.
To a friend, your heart.
To a customer, service.
To all, charity.
To every child, a good example.
To yourself, respect."

Oren Arnold

The Light of Life

Candy Abbott

"God has delivered me from going down to the pit,
And I shall live to enjoy the light of life."
Job 33:28 (NIV)

Few people know that I had a near-death experience a week after my daughter was born. Complications from delivery in 1971 sent me back to the hospital for emergency surgery, and the doctor said afterward, "We almost lost you."

During the operation, I floated down a long, dark hallway, weightless and carefree, conscious only that I existed, similar to how a baby must feel in the womb, unaware of any other living person or thing. It was dark, so very dark, but I knew instinctively that I was loved and in a safe place. Oh, the *love!* If only I had words to describe the depth and completeness of that love. I instinctively knew that I was fully accepted, secure, and carefree—loved with no conditions or expectations. But, truly, words fail me to impart the reality of my awareness of that love.

My time in the tunnel is as real to me today as when it happened forty-plus years ago. I vividly recall a tiny pinprick of light catching my attention and drawing me forward. I floated leisurely toward it. There was no sense of time or place, just "being."

I curled myself into a ball and rolled forward in a straight line, as though I were a bowling ball. For variety, I zigzagged while rolling until I tired of that and resumed a steady, slow roll. Then, I relaxed again and continued floating in a state of timelessness as before, but became aware that I had appendages attached to the sides of me, which I could extend and move upward and downward. So, I began flapping my arms, slowly at first and then faster, faster, faster, until they were blurred like a hummingbird's wings. With this newfound freedom, I became cognizant of another set of limbs at the bottom of me that I could also move at will. Pretty soon I was doing jumping jacks, up and down, faster and faster. And then I floated some more, always forward, never back.

Then the calculations began in my mind. In the real world, I am no mathematician. But in this experience, I was a genius. It started with one single thing, like a human cell, which I watched divide itself in half. Then those two halves began dividing and interacting with one another, multiplying, dividing, and multiplying again—I guess some sort of calculus. My mind kept track of every single detail, understanding and comprehending not only what was transpiring, but the relational aspect of how each unique cell fit together and impacted the others.

With no warning whatsoever, it was like someone flipped a switch, and everything jolted into reverse—like a film rewinding.

The numbers and cells retracted, the jumping jacks and hummingbird arm-flaps reversed, I floated backward, un-zigzagged and unrolled, floated back to where it all began, and awoke with a start to find a nurse's face staring into mine.

Everything was so bright, I had to squint to see. The power of the adventure I'd experienced was so strong, I had to tell her about this wonderful place I'd been yanked away from. I managed to say, "I was just down a long hallway," before closing my eyes. Instantly, I was back there again, in that secure place with no pain or bright lights or sound—only unconditional, abiding love.

A second time, my eyes opened, and I saw a nurse standing over me. "I was just down a long hallway," I said, and again closed my eyes and willed myself back to that serene place. I didn't want to leave.

The third time I opened my eyes, the nurse said, "I know, I know. You were just down a long hallway." And from that time on, I could never go back.

Twenty years later, when I was sharing this with a friend and got to the part about the math, she said, "Candy, don't you see? The Lord has a plan and a purpose for each of us. This was a vision of the lives the Lord planned to touch through you and how those lives, in turn, would affect so many others!"

Whatever it meant, I am convinced that I was heaven-bound that day, moving toward the light of heaven, but God delivered me to enjoy the light of life in this world. As my family and I celebrated Christmas in 1971, I remember rocking, with my daughter on my lap, and giving thanks to God for the gift of life—Christ's, my baby's, and my own.

Since then, heaven has become very real to me.

And do you know what the Lord is saying? That He wants us to be ready to meet Him at any moment. That He's coming soon.

Are you ready? What do you need to do to be ready? Maybe it is to simply be aware that His light shines within you.

Lord, You are the Light of Life. Thank You for delivering us from the pit of sin and darkness and putting us on the pathway of love and light. We are grateful, Lord, for each breath we draw and the opportunity to learn and practice Your ways until the day comes for You to take us to heaven.

Where Are You, Christmas?

Pam Halter

After Jesus was born in Bethlehem in Judea,
during the time of King Herod,
Magi from the East came to Jerusalem and asked,
"Where is the one who has been born king of the Jews?"
Matthew 2:1-2 (NIV)

When they remade *How the Grinch Stole Christmas*, I felt irritated. The Grinch is my favorite Christmas cartoon, rivaled only by Charlie Brown. I wasn't going to watch it, but curiosity got the best of me. And guess what? I loved it!

As Hollywood does, it took a few artistic liberties. One of the additions was a song called "Where Are You, Christmas?" Little Cindy-Lou is searching for the real meaning of Christmas, which seems to be getting lost in the shuffle. When I listened to the words of her lament, it seemed to me that I was also lost in the shuffle of gift-buying, cookie-baking, decorating the house and endless holiday programs to attend. I, too, wondered, "Where Are You, Christmas?"

God's Word tells us the story of the first Christmas. The real Christmas. How wonderful that God gave us His Son, a baby born in a stable, who would grow to be King of Kings and Lord of Lords. Knowing that pulls me out of the shuffle and sets me on solid ground.

Lord Jesus, You are the real meaning of Christmas. Help me find You in the midst of my Grinches and Charlie Browns so I may worship You.

The Crèche

David Michael Smith

"Let the little children come to me,
and do not hinder them,
for the kingdom of God belongs to such as these."
Luke 18:16 (NIV)

Right after Thanksgiving, it begins. Families and couples, people of all ages and backgrounds, begin their annual pilgrimage to the local Christmas tree farm to tag the "perfect tree" for the upcoming festive, yuletide season. At Turning Pointe Farm near Hartly, Delaware, tagging trees is commonplace. But miracles? Well, *that's* what makes the holiday season so magical.

Born and raised in New York City and later residents of northern New Jersey, Tom and Roseann Conlon were familiar with traffic gridlock, high crime rates, even higher taxes, and a lifestyle that was far from tranquil. So, in 1986, they purchased thirty-six acres of wooded farmland in the fertile epicenter of Delaware and became part-time, weekend farmers.

After building a cozy log cabin on their own slice of earthly heaven, they diligently planted 3,000 evergreen seedlings by hand the first year and named their picturesque tree farm "Turning Pointe Farm." For nearly two decades they farmed the rich, flat acreage. They planted additional firs, pines, and spruces until the fields were filled with beautiful boughs of greenery and a harvest of trees that had matured to marketable heights.

After retiring in 2003, the Conlons moved to their Delaware farm and realized their long-time dream to operate their Christmas tree farm full time. With more time to work the land, trim and sell trees, and assemble beautiful wreaths and holiday centerpieces, Turning Pointe Farm became a place that brings broad smiles of joy to those who patronized their farm every chilly December.

But it wasn't until they put up the annual crèche in 2004 that things got *really* interesting. The Conlons and their son-in-law built a platform and a three-sided rustic shelter, covered with greenery grown on the farm, for the nearly life-sized figurines. Each piece was made of resin that resembled natural stone, consisting of: a welcoming, watchful angel; the precious, sleeping infant Jesus; His earthly parents, a noble Joseph and a kneeling, prayerful Mary; a young shepherd with his sheep, all adoring the holy child; and the three Magi, patiently awaiting turns to present their gifts. The holy scenery was breath stealing to all eyes.

The inspiration behind the manger came from Roseann. She wanted to bring the "reason for the season" to tangible, meaningful life for her six grandchildren and keep the holiday's focus on the virgin birth of the Son of God. So, the day after Thanksgiving, the Conlon grandchildren carefully carried the plastic participants to the manger and set up the nativity. Then they added a large stone to the display with the word "Blessings" carved in it.

After the nativity scene was erected, Roseann and her husband told tree shoppers about the display. People, if they felt led to do so, could go to the manger and silently offer up their prayer requests. And many did. At the same time, her grandchildren, ranging in ages from three to eleven, prayed daily for all the people and their petitions. For the young prayer warriors, it was a faith maturing ministry of good will during the season known for good will.

The Conlon grandchildren didn't often know the exact requests since they were offered privately, but on occasion, someone would mention their need to Roseann. The family prayed for people struggling with cancer, sickness, and disease. They prayed for broken relationships. They prayed for people suffering depression, a common ailment during the holiday season. But one desperate plea at the crèche stood out that first year . . .

Eric and Stephanie lived nearby and had frequented the farm in the past. They were a young couple, married for ten years, with no children. But they wanted them. In fact, their hearts ached for children, but for nearly a decade nothing worked. They tried every off-the-wall piece of advice from friends, neighbors, and family. They tried ovulation kits. They tried fertility drugs. They tried medical procedures like In Vitro Fertilization and artificial insemination in an effort to have a baby and start a family. And they prayed for a miracle, *their* miracle, one about seven or eight pounds in weight, twenty inches in length, with rosy cheeks and a quick smile. But absolutely nothing worked.

To deepen and intensify the mournful depression the couple was battling, Stephanie's mother was also very sick with cancer. The prognosis was shrouded in darkness, without the light of life. Stephanie had always hoped her mother would live long enough to hold her grandchild and smile into the eyes of the joyous bundle who would one day carry on the family heritage. But it appeared this hope was an improbable, wishful fantasy.

As the couple picked out a Christmas tree, a Douglas fir, striking and statuesque, they quietly made their way to the manger scene.

Roseann watched from afar and diverted foot traffic away while the hurting woman and her husband clasped hands and reverently bowed their heads. The Christ child in the crib seemed to reach upward toward the husband and wife, as if to welcome their petitions and praise. They were only there for a few minutes, and then they left. No one knew of their prayer appeal, no one except God.

Christmas came and went, and day by day, the year passed. Soon it was frigid and cold again, winter once more on earth's stage, and the excitement of Christmas was gently energizing the season.

Roseann was in her gift shop, the Evergreen Spirit, working on holiday wreaths when the door opened. It was the familiar couple, Eric and Stephanie, another year older, but at once noticeably different. They appeared radiant, even glowing, and seemed taller, as if they had grown like the hundreds of evergreens at Turning Pointe Farm. They bustled into the shop and began blurting out a story, a "miracle." The words were unnecessary, though, because when Stephanie's heavy woolen coat parted, Roseann could see that Stephanie was quite pregnant!

"We prayed for a baby at your nativity last year," Stephanie said with tears in her eyes. "We were distraught, but standing there looking down on Jesus, we felt something . . . hope."

Roseann embraced the happy couple, squeezed them hard, and explained the motivation behind assembling the crèche, which was back up for the new Christmas season. She told the soon-to-be parents about her grandchildren's faithful prayers—intercessory pleas made to the Creator on the behalf of total strangers.

"And guess when I'm due?" Stephanie added with a grin.

Roseann, still overwhelmed by the blissful news, couldn't answer, so Eric blurted out, "Christmas! December 25th!"

When the faith of little children, or those who come as children, is on display, God Himself cannot remain idle. Miracles, healings, blessings, and acts of wonder become the norm. Just ask Eric and Stephanie, and they'll gladly tell you all about their handsome little boy, the best Christmas gift they will ever know!

The Most Precious Gift of All

Wilma Shepard Caraway

The most precious gift of all—Jesus!
Exalt Him! As most everyone's thoughts turn to Jesus,
We reflect on His miraculous birth in Bethlehem.
He is our resurrected Savior,
Whose life was sacrificed
In order to save you and me from our sins
So we can have everlasting life.
Christmas is the time of year when we sing carols and
Happy Birthday to Jesus Who died on the cross and
Who rose from the dead on the third day.
He is the son of God incarnate.
Jesus was born to the Virgin Mary.
The Good Shepherd will return to earth to fulfill the Word.
He is the Trinity—the Father, Son, and Holy Spirit.
He is the Messiah and our Savior.
If you have not already done so,
Ask Jesus to come into your heart so that you will be saved.
You will receive the most precious gift of all—Jesus!

*For God so loved the world that he gave his one and only Son,
that whoever believes in him shall not perish but have eternal life.
John 3:16 (NIV)*

By His Grace

Michele Jones

The prophets proclaimed Him so long ago
His life foreshadowed within each scroll
The long-awaited Messiah
Who will soon come.
And with Him,
Justice He will bring.
A mighty King to set us free,
He will be our King, our Prince of Peace.

How strange for such a coming king in a manger to lay,
A trough carved of stone where animals eat grain
Wrapped in torn cloth, not fine linens or silk
No pillow or bed,
A child-king with no jeweled crown for his head
No pomp or parade,
Born of lowly estate
Flesh-encased deity
Born to walk the earth with man
To glorify the Father and personify redemption's plan.

A child-king with no jeweled crown for His head
But a God Child who chose a crown of thorns instead
Who allowed the temple veil to be torn
What was once secret, now made known
His life was meant to ransom our souls

The manger didn't stop Him
The cross couldn't keep Him
Death couldn't hold Him
For he is risen and is coming again!
This is what we celebrate when we remember His birth
God incarnate, coming to earth
A Messiah King born into this world
Of humble beginnings
And the same Messiah Savior
Who, for us, will soon return.

Did It Hurt?

Candy Abbott

He who testifies to these things says,
"Yes, I am coming soon."
Amen.
Come, Lord Jesus.
Revelation 22:20 (NIV)

Oh, the joy of opening those beautifully wrapped gifts on Christmas morning! Among the squeals of delight and warm thank-yous, the sacrifices we made of time and money are quickly forgotten. But there is one Sacrifice that we will want to take a moment to remember.

Recently, I saw a picture that I can't get out of my mind. It was a painting of a young girl looking up at Jesus who was dressed in white with His hands outstretched toward her, revealing the nail prints from His crucifixion. Beneath the picture, in a child's scrawl, were the words, "Did it hurt?" The question took my breath away.

Jesus, did it hurt to leave the glories of heaven to clothe Yourself in human flesh? Did it hurt to struggle through the bumps and bruises of childhood so You would know firsthand what it was like to grow up in the world You created for us? Did it hurt when people You came to rescue from sin not only refused to listen but mocked and nailed You to a Roman cross?

To the little girl in the picture, thank you for reminding us, as we celebrate the birth of the Christ child, that the greatest gift of Christmas is Immanuel (God with us).

Jesus left the eternal perfection of heaven to come and live among us in our pain-filled world . . . so that we who believe in Jesus may one day leave this pain-filled world to go and live with Him in the eternal perfection of heaven.

$$\infty$$

Thank You, Lord, for giving until it hurt. Thank You for coming as an infant, for growing up as our Savior, and for promising to come back to receive us unto Yourself. Of all the gifts we have ever received, we love You the best. Come, Lord Jesus. Come again, soon!

Wrap It Up!

Jean Davis

As I wrapped a gift for our son's friend Amy, I had trouble getting the paper cut exactly straight. What was wrong with those scissors? Packages we received from others were always wrapped perfectly. As I struggled with comparisons of perfection and my inadequacies, I laughed out loud as a memory of another wrapped package came to mind.

Right before Christmas, our daughter invited us and our friend Diana for supper. Before Diana arrived, our daughter began wrapping a present for her. She cut the paper to fit. As she left her scissors, paper, box and tape on the floor to answer the phone, she turned to Olivia, her four-year-old, and said sternly, "Leave everything there. Let Mommy do it."

Mommy was hardly out of the room before Olivia began to wrap the package herself.

"Olivia," I said. "Remember what Mommy said about leaving everything alone?"

"Mmmhhmmm," Olivia said as her busy fingers scrunched and smoothed the pretty paper.

Well, who needed a square box to be square with the paper? So what if the box wasn't entirely covered? Who cared if a triangle of paper sticking straight out at one edge called attention to itself? Olivia gave the package concentrated effort during our daughter's five minute phone call and wrapped the package with great love and enthusiasm. She pulled one square of tape after another off the dispenser and applied it to one end of the box. She was satisfied with her wrapping job only when all the tape on the dispenser was gone.

Our daughter came back into the room just as Diana knocked on the door, so there was no time for any scolding or rewrapping. I don't remember now what the gift was, but I do remember the gift wrap. As Diana hugged Olivia, she said she *loved* the gift and especially the wrapping job.

Maybe it's time I quit making comparisons. Amy may not care if the paper edges aren't cut exactly straight and the tape is applied a little lopsided. Perhaps she'll love the gift, or possibly she'll look at our son and say knowingly, "Aw, I bet your mother wrapped this all by herself, bless her heart."

Kinsman Redeemer

Cheri Fields

"Think not that I am come to destroy the law, or the prophets:
I am not come to destroy, but to fulfil."
Matthew 5:17 (KJV)

But when the fulness of the time was come,
God sent forth his Son, made of a woman, made under the law,
to redeem them that were under the law,
that we might receive the adoption of sons.
Galatians 4:4-5 (KJV)

We often talk of Mary's great faith, but what was at stake if Joseph had refused to obey God's command through the angel?

Jesus came to earth not to do away with the good deeds of the law, but to perfectly fulfill the law of God as given to Moses. In the Sermon on the Mount, Jesus says this plainly. His whole life was lived in obedience to what God had told His people so many years before.

Psalm 40:6-8 talks about how Jesus would come and give His life as a sacrifice that would please God.

Hebrews 10 quotes this Psalm and continues on to tell us that this is why Jesus only had to die one time.

First Corinthians 15:45 tells us that Jesus had to have no human father to be born without a sin nature, but he needed to have a surrogate father in order to fulfill the law.

Deuteronomy 23:2 lists a harsh command against out-of-wedlock children in Jewish society. Without Joseph's decision to claim Jesus as his own, Jesus would have been barred from the temple and unable to participate in Jewish life. He would have been an outcast from the people of God. Thank God, Joseph did obey God's commands!

Through Jesus' sacrifice, we too can perfectly fulfill the Law, no matter what is in our past. (See Romans 8:4.)

Dear Jesus, thank You for coming to earth to be our Kinsman Redeemer. Thank You for fulfilling the law of God so perfectly that we don't have to match You to be in Your family. Please take my life and make it pleasing to You as a living sacrifice of praise.

Christmas Is for Children

Leslie F. Claunch

Jesus said,
"Let the little children come to me, and do not hinder them,
for the kingdom of God belongs to such as these."
Matthew 19:14 (NIV)

Christmas is for children—
not just the little humans, but childlike ones of all ages,
of whom Jesus comprises His kingdom.

Christmas is a time of joy—
when we all remember what it is to be a kid and
maintain a childlike faith, no matter what.

Christmas is a reminder—
that Jesus came to show us how to live and love. He
did not remain the baby in the manger, that we always
depict Him this time of the year. He was and is and ever
shall be, the Lord and Savior of the universe. When He
permeates your being, every day is Christmas.

Jesus, teach me to be your witness and to live my life to Your glory, through
this season and always.

Christmas Word Search

Compiled by
Wilma Shepard Caraway

The following list of words is related to Christmas. See how many of the hidden words you can find in the diagram. The words are always in a straight line and may read up, down, forward, backward, or diagonally. Cross the word off the list once you have circled it. Some words may overlap.

MERRY	FRIENDS	COOKIES
CHRISTMAS	CAROLS	STAR
MISTLELTOE	RUDOLPH	MARY
LIGHTS	CRIB	JOSEPH
GIFTS	BULBS	BIRTHDAY
BABY	POINSETTIA	HOME
JESUS	CARDS	GIVE
MANGER	SANTA	LOVE
TOYS	TREE	FUN
EAST	BELLS	WISE
PRESENTS	MILK	MEN
FAMILY	INN	FOOD
SNOW	HOLLY	NOEL

Ready? Sharpen your pencil and begin! *(No peeking at the answer key until you're finished.)*

E	M	I	S	T	L	E	T	O	E	E	W	I	S	E
O	S	E	A	N	U	F	O	O	D	A	C	B	U	H
R	T	Q	R	P	Z	B	Y	H	A	S	A	U	P	M
W	H	I	J	R	E	T	S	O	U	T	R	L	X	E
Y	G	I	V	E	Y	L	I	M	A	F	O	B	R	N
G	I	F	T	S	T	C	L	E	M	D	L	S	H	D
K	L	N	O	E	L	N	H	O	U	C	S	N	O	W
F	R	I	E	N	D	S	Z	R	V	G	I	A	L	U
C	R	I	B	T	B	A	B	Y	I	E	N	F	L	T
M	D	L	T	S	E	J	E	S	U	S	N	W	Y	C
I	B	I	R	T	H	D	A	Y	E	S	T	A	R	A
L	V	B	E	L	L	S	R	E	G	N	A	M	S	R
K	M	H	E	P	O	I	N	S	E	T	T	I	A	D
C	O	O	K	I	E	S	L	S	A	N	T	A	E	S
M	A	R	Y	O	A	N	D	O	J	O	S	E	P	H

Love was born
on
Christmas
morn

Waiting

Barry A. Jones

God is not a man, that he should lie;
neither the son of man, that he should repent:
hath he said, and shall he not do it?
Or hath he spoken, and shall he not make it good?

Numbers 23:19 (KJV)

It will never be found on anyone's list of favorite things to do. It could even be termed one of life's most difficult tasks. We all participate in it to varying degrees on a daily basis. What is it? Waiting!

What are you waiting for? How long have you been waiting for it? More importantly, what is your attitude while you wait?

When I think of Christmas, it's always with the thought of waiting. As the season approaches, there's anticipation that so permeates the atmosphere that it's almost tangible.

I think of the multitudes that have waited throughout the years for the fulfillment of God's promise. I also think about the importance of our attitude while we wait. Israel waited for forty-two generations to see that promise fulfilled through the Christ child. Many Jewish people still wait because the promise didn't come the way they expected. Because of that, they didn't recognize the promise when it arrived.

Elizabeth and Zachariah joined all of Israel in waiting for the coming of the Messiah. They waited so long that they gave up on their personal hope for a son. Though it appeared their desire would never be manifested, they continued to serve God with their whole being. He rewarded them by granting their hearts' desire. He blessed them with a son and made him the forerunner of the Christ.

After Mary received Gabriel's message that she would be the mother of the Christ child, we aren't told how long she had to wait for the Holy Spirit to overshadow her. After it happened, like all expectant mothers, she had to wait nine months for the baby's birth. I'm sure there were times that she felt inadequate and unworthy, but God makes no mistake in whom He chooses for any given task. He had equipped her for the responsibility that he placed in her hands.

The wise men had to wait. They knew the prophecies regarding the birth of the Messiah. They not only had to prepare for their journey, they had to leave all that was familiar. Being from "the East," probably Persia or modern-day Iran, they would have had to travel 800 or 900 miles to see the young child and His parents. They didn't know when they would get back home or what the cost would be. They only knew that they had to be obedient to what God placed in their hearts.

Does it seem that you've been waiting a long time for what God has promised you? He is faithful to bring every Word that He has spoken to pass. His promises are yea and, in Him, Amen. Continue to trust Him. When the time is right, He will bring it to pass.

$$\infty$$

Father, Your timing is always perfect. Help me to be patient as I wait on You.

Two Christmas Gifts

Anna Buckler

After my ophthalmologist chewed me up and spit me out with "black news," my faith, as well as my holiday spirit, was shot. What was this news that rocked my world? Apparently, the report he had received from my neurosurgeon called my situation an "emergency" that required immediate intervention. He informed me that the Delaware Association for the Blind offered benefits for those with vision problems—like a seeing eye dog!

You must understand that I'm presently blind in my right eye and have lost a good deal of peripheral vision in my left eye. Both eye conditions are due to aneurysms.

My dear husband, David, was privy to all this. In an effort to cheer me up, he decided we needed to go to Hardee's for breakfast. I love their biscuits and gravy. We headed off and, once there, I had to go to the restroom.

As I stepped inside, I saw a woman in a Home Health Aide uniform drying her hands, so I greeted her with "God bless you!" And we started talking. I'm not exactly sure how we bypassed the typical restroom small talk, but suddenly we were discussing aneurysms. She shared that her son was recovering from a brain aneurysm that resulted in surgery with minor problems, but overall, he was doing well.

Then from the bathroom stall, the voice of another woman chimed in to say that she, too, had survived aneurysm surgery and had come through it just fine.

I couldn't believe it! What are the odds that those two women, having firsthand experience with aneurysms, would be in the restroom of a fast food restaurant at that precise moment? And isn't it interesting that no other woman came in to interrupt my holy encounter with them? Were they angels? I believe so—angels with comforting words, strong embraces, and one message that will stay with me forever: "Encouragement."

Maybe I did need an emergency intervention, after all—but not in the form of a seeing-eye dog. No, the God of miracles orchestrated a *divine* intervention for me.

I chuckle when I think about how the Lord delights in surprising us, like choosing for His own birthplace a lowly manger stall instead of a kingly palace. Isn't it just like Him to lead me to a modern-day stall and give me not one but two Christmas gifts in the privacy of a public restroom?

Isn't This Supposed to be About Christmas?

Michele Jones

He released the man who had been thrown into prison for insurrection and murder, the one they asked for, and surrendered Jesus to their will. As they [the soldiers] led him away, they seized Simon from Cyrene, who was on his way in from the country, and put the cross on him and made him carry it behind Jesus. A large number of people followed him, including women who mourned and wailed for him.

Luke 23:25-27 (NIV)

Hey! Wait a minute. Isn't this supposed to be about Christmas? The crucifixion doesn't have anything to do with Christmas.

Oh, my friend, it does. You see, without the birth, death, burial, and resurrection of our Lord and Savior, Jesus Christ, there would be no reason to celebrate Christmas. It would just be another day—another square block on a calendar. It would only be time with no meaning or life without any purpose or hope.

Christmas is interwoven in the crucifixion. For Christ *purposed* (that is, He *chose*) to come to earth in the form of His creation in order to make restoration for us with our heavenly Father. It was His birth leading to His ultimate death on the cross that provided a way of salvation for all of mankind. We can live in victory in this life and the next because Jesus is alive. The grave could not keep Him. He has risen! That is why the Christmas celebration is so special.

This Christmas season, don't just smile at the tiny baby lying in a manger. Look again and see our great King smiling back at us. Merry Christmas!

⁓

I have been crucified with Christ and I no longer live, but Christ lives in me. The life I now live in the body, I live by faith in the Son of God, who loved me and gave himself for me (Galatians 2:20 NIV).

White Spruce from Heaven

David Michael Smith

Seldom do you find a good tree story. There's Shel Silverstein's *"The Giving Tree."* Then there's that tale about George Washington and the cherry tree. And the Bible offers the documented, eyewitness account of Jesus cursing the fig tree.

But this is not a story about cursed trees. Rather, it is a true story about a *blessed* tree, a traditional Christmas icon, and one that brought supernatural, inconceivable blessings to a family in Delaware.

"Mom?"

The voice on the phone was tentative, a young man. The question wasn't intended for identification since he already knew it was his mother, but more to gauge her temperament. He was calling with bad news from distant lands.

"Ephraim!" she breathed with excitement. Then she paused, a mother's barometric intuition rising from within her maternal DNA. "What's wrong?"

Ephraim Rogers, a thin, sandy-haired man in his middle twenties, was an award-winning soldier in the Delaware Army National Guard's Military Police (MP) 153rd Unit. He was the first Army National Guard soldier to have ever won the Army's

"Soldier of the Quarter Award" twice. He was ordered to Riyadh, in central Saudi Arabia, in July 2002, just prior to the roll out of *Operation Iraqi Freedom*, leaving behind a loving and faithful family in Dover, Delaware. His unit's primary mission was to provide security for the American airbase located in Riyadh. The unit was projected to return to the states in March 2003, but there was growing hope that the soldiers could return home for the holidays.

"Things are kind of edgy over here, Mom," Ephraim replied with a serious tone. "I can't get into it, you know, classified security stuff. I'm sure it's in the news back home every night."

"You're not coming home for Christmas, are you?" she asked, already knowing the answer.

"Still hoping for March, Mom. It was a long shot for Christmas, you know?"

"Yes," she managed, her hopes dashed.

After a pause, he asked, "Did you get my presents?" His voice carried an upbeat tenor.

"Yes, they came today, several large boxes, all wrapped. You did a good job. Who helped you?" She laughed.

"No one, Mom," Ephraim replied lightheartedly. "I wrapped them myself." Then after an awkward period of silence, "Mom, I got to run. Probably won't talk to you 'til after the holidays so please tell everyone 'Merry Christmas' for me, okay? I'll e-mail when I can, but they're keeping us busy."

The mother couldn't talk, her throat constricted, tears pooled in her eyes.

"I love you, Mom." Then the call ended.

It was only a mere two weeks until Christmas Eve. Earlier that same week, Lilian Rogers, the soldier's mother, in preparation for her son's possible homecoming, visited nearby Turning Pointe Farm and selected a striking and splendid White Spruce. The bluish-green needled conifer was immediately decorated with the family ornaments, twinkling lights, and some tinsel. It was perfectly shaped, and delivered a visual and aromatic air of Christmas to the house. Ephraim's gifts were strategically placed under the tree's branches where additional gifts would soon join them.

Christmas was quietly and reverently celebrated by the Rogers family, minus Ephraim, but Lilian, after discussing the idea with her husband, Al, and their daughters, Corinne and Louise, decided that all gifts would remain unopened until Ephraim's safe homecoming. The family watered the cut tree throughout the Epiphany season, often referred to as the "12 Days of Christmas," and for the rest of January. And then they stopped, in view of taking it down.

But as the calendar days clicked away and February came and went, the family witnessed a strange, unexplainable reality . . . the White Spruce had not lost any needles. It continued to look as fresh as the day the majestic tree was sawed down in the field, tenderly carried into the house and erected in the emerald and burgundy colored tree stand the family had used for decades.

With a sparkle in their eyes and sympathetic hearts, Corinne and Louise suggested the tree remain in place as long as it continued to look good and retained its needles. They reasoned,

"Why take it down?" But they also assumed the tree was on its last leg, especially since they continued to deprive the tree of any watery nourishment.

In the interim, they decided to also add yellow ribbons and bows to the branches in preparation of Ephraim's return in March. And each night they plugged in the lights. Could the tree miraculously hold on?

The deployment for the soldiers of the 153rd Delaware Army National Guard unit was about to end, and excitement connected the First State to the sandy landscapes of Saudi Arabia when the second Iraqi War violently broke out. Evil ambitioned terrorists in Riyadh blew up a hotel where many Americans were staying as guests. Ephraim's unit was summoned to assist in removing the deceased. The work was solemnly and carefully completed, but tensions in the region were understandably high. Ephraim, and his dedicated buddies stood guard in full military armor and garb for shifts lasting 14 hours in 120 degrees of suffocating heat. It was a hellish existence, and Ephraim, along with many of his fellow soldiers, relied on prayer and faith in God to survive the challenging days.

No one went home in March, as their deployment was extended.

April arrived, and brought with it the season of spring, a time of renewal and rebirth, both in the earth's soil and in the hearts of mankind. Still, the Christmas tree stood proudly in the Rogers' home like a protective sentry, as did Ephraim and his unit at a barricaded gate in the Middle East. Not one needle had fallen from any of the branches. The miracle continued.

Ephraim's unit did eventually come home on the tenth of *May!* They were embraced with a hero's welcome when they landed, complete with tears of joy and bear hugs from joyous family members, all captured by local TV stations and newspaper columnists and photographers. The homecoming festivities spilled over to the Rogers household as Christmas gifts were happily shredded open to reveal items purchased by Ephraim for his family while stationed at Riyadh, including diamonds for his sisters and expensive cigars for Dad. Laughter filled the house, Christmas carols wafted through the stereo speakers, cameras captured each precious moment, while outside the neighbors mowed grass and planted bulbs.

That evening, the tree was taken down and placed outside. Not one needle ever fell from its limbs. The family stood in awe, and praised God. Then everyone went to bed, exhausted but ecstatic.

Lilian walked outside the next morning and took in the beauty of the morning; singing birds busy at work on nests and hunting worms, the fragrant scents of freshly cut grass and sprouting flowers, and the warmth of rich, yellow sunshine upon her face. Then she noticed the tree. It had changed. It had *really* changed.

In less than twelve hours, the green fir tree had turned orangey brown as if it had been dead for months. The needles were dried out, crispy, and many of them, hundreds, now littered the ground. Lilian was amazed. Was this the same tree that looked as good last night as it did five months ago when it was taken from Turning Pointe Farm?

And were those heaven-bound angels that stealthily departed the Rogers' residence in the middle of the night, upon spacious, lucent wings? Angels that also enveloped Ephraim and his peers with holy protection and stood proudly beside them at the Air Force base in Riyadh? Angels from an army above the highest clouds and earth's firmament, acting on the prayers of a believing family and commands from the One, and at the center, a simple, divine Christmas tree, a White Spruce from heaven.

The Most Influential Man

Candy Abbott

Drew and I were driving along and came to a red light where we noticed a license plate with an interesting arrangement of numbers. This triggered a discussion of the complexities and 100% accuracy of the numerical system that God created. Our conversation led us to appreciate the ability that God has placed within human beings to decipher numbers and to make sense of written alphabets. From the visual of the license plate, we observed the sunset and were discussing the complexities of the eyes to appreciate beauty and the ears to hear and interpret sound. We were fully basking in the enormity and wonders of the Master of the Universe when the light turned green.

Drew seemed particularly pensive. "Other than Jesus Christ," he said, "who is the one man with the most influence?"

"Adam?" I asked.

"No," he said.

Trying to think like Drew would think, I guessed again. "Billy Graham?"

"No." He glanced at me with a puzzled look. "It's not that hard. I can't believe you didn't get it the first time."

"The one man with the most influence . . . in the whole world . . . since the beginning of time?" I asked.

"Yes," he said and waited while I thought, to no avail.

"I give up," I admitted. "Who?"

"Santa Claus!"

The Unopened Gift

Catherine L. Young

The unopened gift sat mocking her as if to say, *Why did you bother? He hasn't kept a promise to you in years.* Tears fell silently along her cheek, dripping off her chin. She longed for her eldest son to return. He had called just last week to say he'd be home for Christmas. It would have been his first visit in years, but alas, he was a no-show and hadn't even called to let her know he was okay. This wasn't the first time a gift sat mocking her hope, but it would be her last. For her, time was running out.

This is similar to the parable of the prodigal son—a father hoping for the return of his wayward son. How sad that this cycle is as prevalent in modern times as it was when Jesus told the story.

But my question this Christmas is to you, the reader. Have you left Father God's gift on the table, mocking Him? Or have you unwrapped and embraced the gift of Jesus Christ as your Lord and Savior?

Time is short. Daily, we see signs that End Times prophecies are being fulfilled before our very eyes. The day of Christ's return is nearer now than ever before. Go ahead—open your gift! Accept Jesus, and move forward into the fullness of life only He can give. Simply bow your head, humble your heart, and ask Christ to enter in and take up residence in your mind, will, and emotions.

Celebrate His birth this season. Happy Birthday Jesus!

Great Is the Company

Lori Ciccanti

Suddenly a great company of the heavenly host
appeared with the angel, praising God and saying,
"Glory to God in the highest,
and on earth peace to men on whom His favor rests."
Luke 2:13-14 (NIV)

The voices of about three thousand college students, including my son and daughter, singing the words to the song, *Lion of Judah* by Paul Wilbur, is one of the most inspiring anthems of praise I have ever heard. Listening to the recording of these beautiful voices united in worship brings to mind the magnificent angelic praise of the heavenly host which did announce the blessed birth of our Savior and Lord.

Through the proclamation of angels, the Lord revealed His glory to a few humble shepherds the very first Christmas morning. By way of illustration, Daniel 10:6 describes the voice of just one angel as being like that of "a multitude." So with that thought in mind, can you imagine the awesome sound of this heavenly choir which was sent to declare the Messiah's birth?

An interesting debate among Bible scholars leaves me wondering whether or not angels do sing. Since there are only two references in Scripture referring to angels singing (Job 38:7 and Revelation 5:11-12), some believe they sang before the fall and will one day sing again when all creation has been redeemed.

Nonetheless, the voice power of many angels praising God in one accord expresses the highest form of reverence, worship, and devotion to God. With the great company of the redeemed on earth, may our voices join with the holy angels to resonate the glory of God with sacred music and spiritual songs moving our hearts to honor Him whose Word we do proclaim.

Father, during this special Advent season, may our voices be heard throughout the world proclaiming the Messiah's birth to the praise and glory of Your name, through Jesus Christ our Lord.

Nativity Scenes

Leslie F. Claunch

For unto us a Child is born,
Unto us a Son is given;
And the government will be upon His shoulder.
And His name will be called
Wonderful, Counselor, Mighty God,
Everlasting Father, Prince of Peace.
Isaiah 9:6 (NKJV)

Among my most prized possessions are my Nativity Scenes. I have several different kinds. I even put a small ceramic one that I found at Dollar General on the window sill of one of my bathrooms. I have one made of olive wood. It was imported from The Holy Land and found its way to the church bazaar. My mother bought it for me for my birthday. I like to set it up on the sideboard, because the wood is the same color and it looks like figurines are growing out of the sideboard. There is the one made with snowy white figurines that are set on an oval shaped piece of wood and grace the drop leaf table, but my pride and joy is the one that is so totally biblically correct.

I have collected pieces during my entire lifetime, and I think I finally have it completed. When I was a small child, you could buy Nativity Scenes piece by piece from the various bins of the Five and Dime store. I remember when my daddy and I were picking out the pieces and he told me, "We want to get these camels and wise men that are walking instead of kneeling down with the shepherds, because they came later." We even found one of the wise men who had his hand raised over his eyes as if he was looking at the star. When we took our treasures home, Daddy went to his workshop and built a stable. I was fascinated by the song *The Friendly Beasts,* so he made a rafter in the stable for the doves to perch.

There is a diverse conglomeration of angels that I have accumulated over the years. There are some that were found in my great-grandmother's Victorian ornaments along with a silver eight-point star. There are three ceramic ornaments I made at church camp one year. I think I might have picked up a few at Dollar General. The final set was the one I got at Dollar Tree.

I now have the perfect place for the completed scene. It's in the den on a long shelf. The stable is in the middle and contains the Holy Family, the animals, and some angels. On one side are two shepherds with their sheep and a collie to herd them. On the other side (I made it a point to have them coming from the east) are the wise men and their camels. They are all walking. The wise man with his hand raised is walking in front and looking at the star which I hang on the top cross beam of the shelf. Various angels are arranged on the four shelves below the star. That is the multitude of heavenly hosts praising God and saying, "Glory to God in the highest and peace among men" (Luke 2:14).

All these many and varied pieces seem to fit together perfectly as if to proclaim the diversity of God's creation. To complete the scene takes around thirty minutes because I have to climb up the ladder to the shelf so I can reach each one to put all the angels in their proper places.

I am reminded as I do this of the greatness of God's love that He showed to us with the gift of the Savior—the baby in the manger, and the absolute perfection of this universe He created. Even when I take the scene down at the end of the season, I am still in awe, and I thank Jesus every day.

∞

Father, we thank You for Your gift of the Savior and for everlasting life. Thank You, too, that You never put us on the shelf but are continually available to us throughout the year.

When we were children
we were grateful to those
who filled our stockings at Christmas time.
Why are we not grateful to God
for filling our stockings with legs?

G. K. Chesterton

A Lesson from a Child

Wilma Shepard Caraway

"Keep your lives free from the love of money
and be content with what you have . . ."
Hebrews 13:5 (NIV)

Jenna came running barefoot into our bedroom shouting, "Mommy! Daddy! Get up! It's Christmas! It's time to get up!" I jumped out of bed, grabbed my robe, and ran behind Jenna into the living room.

"Look! Santa ate his cookies, Mommy." Jenna's eyes drifted from the empty plate to our brightly lit Christmas tree and stopped suddenly. The big smile on her face and the sparkle in her eyes faded.

"What's wrong, Honey?"

She walked slowly to the Christmas tree and knelt down. She picked up an orange and what she said next on that Christmas morning broke my heart.

"Just what I wanted, fruit and nuts."

She thinks those are her presents! Jenna didn't cry, scream, or melt into a tantrum, but instead, sat quietly beside the fruit and nuts and gazed on what she perceived to be her Christmas presents.

I burst out, "Sweetheart! Look over there."

Squeals of joy exploded through the house as Jenna discovered the Barbie doll, Barbie Doll house, and other little girl toys that Santa had placed on top of a table out of reach of her curious two-year-old brother, Gerald.

The sparkle returned to her eyes as she lovingly examined each toy.

"Jenna, let's go wake up Daddy and Gerald."

The four of us gathered in the living room by the tree and sang "Silent Night" before opening the wrapped presents, a family tradition.

Jenna threw her arms around me and gave me a big hug and exclaimed, "Mommy, I'm so happy, but I was scared for a little while."

"Why were you scared, Honey?"

"I didn't know how I was going to explain fruit and nuts at Show-and-Tell!"

We all laughed, and I said, "I'm happy you do not have to worry about that now."

∞

Lord Jesus, help us to have the faith of little children and be grateful for the gifts you bestow upon us.

A Celebration Time

Michele Jones

A Celebration Time
Of giving and of sharing
Of laughter and of caring
Of smiles and warm greetings and cheer
Proclaiming it's a wonderful time of year.
What are we celebrating?
Did we feed the poor? Did we help the needy?
Is it God's heart we've been seeking?

It really matters not
The wrapping or the box
It's a matter of the heart
Of which we play such a minuscule part.
See, all along it was God's plan
To redeem man—
to bring us back to Him again
So God became flesh—
He became the carpenter's son.

Joseph, a builder by trade—Jesus the creator of all things,
Refusing to leave us there in the darkness and lost,
The Son constructed a way
Through some nails and a cross
That we might be redeemed and wholly forgiven.

So as we celebrate during this season,
Remember the Christ child is God and King
And in His sovereignty He does still reign.
Whether born in December or born in the spring,
What matters most is that He loved us and came—
He bore our sin, our guilt, our shame,
That we might have fellowship with Him once again

JESUS
He is our gift—sent from above.
He is our wrapping—embracing us with love.
He is our ribbon—tying us to eternity.
He is our carol—the heart song we sing.
He is our glad tiding—Proclaimed by Good News.
He is our Joy—our Hope and our Truth!

Christmas

Judi Folmsbee

"Today in the town of David a Savior has been born to you;
He is Christ the Lord."
Luke 2:11 (NKJV)

I don't know about you, but every year I get frustrated by the event of Christmas being misused and misunderstood. Some people think Christmas is a pagan holiday because some symbols like the Christmas tree were celebrated by pagans in Europe long before anyone heard of the birth of Christ. Others think that Christmas was named after St. Christopher or St. Nicholas.

As we know, Christmas is in honor of the birth of Jesus Christ. The "mas" part of Christmas comes from the Roman Catholic term "mass." Christmas was originally a mass for Christ, to celebrate His birth.

This year, negative publicity in reference to Christians has bothered me more than usual, so I feel compelled to share the real meaning of Christmas, not just in words but in action. In addition to giving to the poor and helping where needed, I am committed to responding with "MERRY CHRISTMAS" when a cashier says, "Happy Holidays." It is my way of standing up to someone who intentionally or unintentionally mocks Christmas.

I was impressed with a piece written by Ben Stein, which aired on his CBS Sunday Morning Commentary:

"I am a Jew, and every single one of my ancestors was Jewish. And it does not bother me even a little bit when people call those beautiful lit up, bejeweled trees, Christmas trees. . . . I don't feel threatened. I don't feel discriminated against. . . . That's what they are, Christmas trees. It doesn't bother me a bit when people say 'Merry Christmas' to me. I don't think they are slighting me or getting ready to put me in a ghetto. In fact, I kind of like it. It shows that we are all brothers and sisters celebrating this happy time of year.

"I don't like getting pushed around for being a Jew, and I don't think Christians like getting pushed around for being Christians. I think people who believe in God are sick and tired of getting pushed around, period. I have no idea where the concept came from that America is an explicitly atheist country. I can't find it in the Constitution, and I don't like it being shoved down my throat."

I pray that we Christians can show more now than ever that Christmas is a blessed event and should not be reduced to a commercial holiday or just a time to get off work. And I think if someone doesn't like the real meaning of Christmas, then they should offer to work the holiday for someone who does.

As for me and my household, we're keeping CHRIST in CHRISTmas. What say you?

*He who has not
Christmas in his heart
will never find it
under a tree.*

Roy L. Smith

Our Founder & Director

Candy Abbott

Founder and director of Delmarva Christian Writers' Fellowship, author, publisher, inspirational speaker, and grandmom, Candy sees herself as a "fruitbearer." Compiling and publishing this book is a labor of love and evidence of her life's goal to exhibit the Fruit of the Spirit (Gal. 5:22-23) in all that she does. She began writing in 1983, around the same time she and a friend co-founded Sisters in Christ, an inter-denominational women's ministry. Candy directs the annual Fruitbearer conference, is a charter member of Southern Delaware Toastmasters, elder and deacon at the Georgetown Presbyterian Church, and president of the Delaware Association of American Mothers. She and her husband Drew own and operate Fruitbearer Publishing, LLC. They have three children and four grandchildren, all in close proximity to their home in Georgetown, Delaware.

She invites you to call her at 302.856.6649, e-mail her at info@fruitbearer.com, or visit one or more of her personal websites:

www.Fruitbearer.com
www.FruitbearEvents.com
www.FruitbearerWebServices.com
www.GavinGoodfellow.com
www.DelmarvaWriters.com

Contributing Authors

Our sincere gratitude to the following members and friends of Delmarva Christian Writers' Fellowship for sharing their inspired words in this volume.

Gail Atlas—Gail's aim in life is to show who God really is, as best as mortal beings can understand Him. She finds great fulfillment as the children's supervisor for Bible Study Fellowship in Milford, as well as serving in church relations for Operation Christmas Child. She loves to read, write, and travel around the country with her husband in their RV. Gail lives in Seaford, Delaware, with her semi-retired husband, Steve. They have four grown children and eight wonderful grandchildren. You can contact her at makarios1225@yahoo.com.

Anna Buckler—Anna is fiercely in love with Jesus. She and her husband, David, have been married seven years and live in Blades, Delaware. They have ten grown children, five in Maryland, two in Massachusetts, one in Tennessee, and two in Florida. This is her first published article, but she is anticipating many more. She worships at Victory Tabernacle Church of God in Laurel. She can be reached at 302.262.0481, 211 E. 7th Street, Blades, DE 19973.

Wilma Shepard Caraway—Wilma compiles quotes and writes articles, poems, and children's stories. Her book, *101 Surprises! Sayings with Scriptures You Didn't See Coming*, was released in September 2012. She is a member of Delmarva Christian Writers' Fellowship and hosts its annual writing retreat at Collins Pond. Wilma is an educator and lifetime honorary member of the Texas Parent and Teacher Association. Wilma resides with her husband, Elton "Lucky" Caraway, in Georgetown, Delaware. They have two children and two grandchildren. She can be reached by e-mail at wiletc@ comcast.net.

Lori Ciccanti—Lori enjoys sharing the Gospel through various forms of writing, teaching Bible studies, and raising awareness for the plight of persecuted Christians. Having a son with autism, she is also involved in ministries for the disabled. Some of her hobbies include: reading inspirational true stories and devotionals, visiting historical sites, collecting dolls, and thrift shopping. Most of all, she enjoys spending time at home with her husband, Lou, three children, and two adorable cats. She can be reached by e-mail at DLAlsina@mchsi.com.

Leslie F. Claunch—Leslie has completed an anthology of her poems and is working on a novel. She attends Georgetown Community Bible Church in Georgetown, Delaware, and is active in Camp Farthest Out and Southern Delaware Toastmasters. Leslie is a mother and grandmother and can be reached at 302.856.7124, lesliemissleslie@aol.com.

Jean Davis—Jean has published devotions in the *Upper Room, Devo'zine, Cup of Comfort Devotional for Women,* and *Love is a Verb Devotional.* Her humorous and inspirational stories have appeared in *Vista, Live, FellowScript, The Heart of a Mother* and

Whispering in God's Ear. She lives in Ocean View, Delaware, with her husband, Vergil. You may contact Jean by e-mail at davis823@mchsi.com.

Malorie Drake Derby—Malorie uses the power of voice and assembly to awaken women to live life full on. She is a wife, mother, grandmother, educator, writer, speaker, and founder of "In Great Company." With more than thirty years' teaching experience, Malorie believes that the Word of God is foundational for all human endeavors and relationships. She is passionate about working with and challenging women to navigate together toward plan and purpose. Contact Malorie at 302.542.1539, mderby8382@gmail.com.

Cheri Fields—Cheri, of Delton Michigan, is a pastor's wife, home schooling mom of five, and aspiring writer for Jesus. She has had an article published and is an active blogger. Interact with Cheri at www.creationscience4kids.com.

Judi Folmsbee—Judi is a retired teacher after twenty-five years in special education classrooms. She has written three children's books. The second edition of *Bubba the Busy Beaver* will be released in 2013. Her work has been published in anthologies, church booklets, and religious and secular newspapers. She enjoys photography, gardening, scrapbooking, family time, and her newest hobby, playing the banjo. Visit Judi at her website, www.JudiFolmsbee.com.

Barbara Creath Foster—A former Delaware teacher and DCWF member, Barbara retired and moved to southwest Florida, where she lives with her oldest son. She's still writing, has completed two inspirational novels. She can be reached by phone at 302.227.2212 or by e-mail at Barbara@StoryWriters.ws.

Faye Green— Faye lives in Middletown, Delaware. She has had three working careers: in the Prince Georges County, Maryland, school system; at Ft. George G. Meade working for the Department of Defense; and as a writer of poetry, fiction, and non-fiction. Her first book of poetry, *Labyrinth,* and a novel, *Dicey,* will be published in 2013. Faye has a short fiction story, *The Boy on the Wall,* on Amazon.com (available digitally). She is a member of St. Paul's United Methodist Church, Odessa, Delaware, and Delmarva Christian Writers' Fellowship, where the Holy Spirit empowers and encourages through Christian Fellowship.

Pam Halter—Pam is a children's author and editor. She also is a contributing author in several devotional books and has ventured into writing nonfiction for parents of special needs children. When she's not writing or reading, she enjoys cooking, gardening, quilting, and Bible study. Pam lives in New Jersey with her husband, Daryl, and two daughters, Anna and Mary. You can read more about Pam on her website: www.PamHalter.com.

Barry A. Jones—Barry was born in Maryland but grew up in Dover, Delaware, and currently resides in Seaford. She has an associate degree in biblical studies from Logos Christian College and Seminary in Jacksonville, Florida. Barry completed a master level voice acting class at Voices for All in Albany, New York, allowing her to fulfill her dream of becoming a voice actor. A wife, mother, and grandmother, relationships are extremely important to her. She is an ordained elder and former pastor. Although most of her career has been in the banking industry, she loves people and desires to encourage others to maximize their God given potential through her life and writing. She may be reached by e-mail at jonesagapegirl@aol.com.

Eddy Jones—Eddy lives in Seaford, Delaware, with his wife, Michele. He holds a Th.D. in Pastoral Theology and has been published in the *Restoration Herald*. He has served in various ministries throughout the Southeast U.S. Currently, he is a teacher at Delmarva Christian High School in Georgetown, Delaware, and part of the leadership team of the Lewes Church of Christ.

Michele Jones—Michele lives in Seaford, Delaware, with her husband, Eddy, and their fun-loving pets. She enjoys her time with her children and is a proud grandmother of three. Accountant by day and writer by night, she thrives in those moments when ink touches page and poetry is born. She also writes devotionals and short stories with a purpose to encourage others to see just how awesome and amazing our God is! She loves to hear from her readers at wordpraise@gmail.com.

Betty Kasperski—Betty is an educator, business leader, certified lay minister, writer, and inspirational speaker. Coming from a family of educators and business owners, she feels comfortable in a variety of settings, including public speaking. Her first book, *Severed Yet Whole*, was released in 2012. She holds a master's degree from Syracuse University and resides in Georgetown, Delaware, with her husband, Stephen. Visit Betty online at www.SeveredYetWhole.com.

Eva C. Maddox—Eva is a graduate of Wright State University and has taken courses in counseling and nursing, as well as several Bible courses through her local church. Eva writes devotions, articles, poems, and stories and has recently completed her first novel. A number of her writings have been published in a variety of Christian publications. In July 2012, she began Kingdom Writers Fellowship, a Christian writers' group that meets monthly in Seaford, Delaware. You may contact her at evacmaddox@comcast.net or check her blog: http://maddoxmatters.wordpress.com.

Kris Penrod—Kris is a grandmother who resides in Seaford, Delaware. Much to her delight, her family moved to the Eastern Shore when she was just a child, enabling her to satisfy her longing for a pony of her own. She has owned horses most of her life and still has two in her pasture. Kris receives her inspiration for writing by finding the "God Moments" in everyday life around her. As the first part of James 4:8 says, "Come near to God and He will come near to you." She believes that glimpses of God can be seen and His voice can be heard in every living thing that He has created, if we will just choose to look and listen. Contact Kris at okpénrod@hotmail.com.

Claire Smith—Claire was born in upper New York. She and her siblings grew up in foster care. Although she started out to be a nurse, she soon discovered that teaching and writing were her true passions. A playwright for twenty-five years, she had also written articles and short stories for adults and children. Claire has a certificate of graduation from Bethany Fellowship Missionary Training School (now Bethany Missionary College), an associate degree in science from Adirondack Community College, a bachelor's degree in secondary education English from the State University of New York in Oneonta, and has completed several post graduate hours. Now retired from teaching, she makes her home on the Eastern Shore of Maryland. Her first book, *Choose to be Chosen,* was released in 2009. Contact Claire at klayre_smith@yahoo.com.

David Michael Smith—David writes from his hometown of Georgetown, Delaware, where he has resided his entire life. He solely credits God for his publishing successes, which includes several appearances in *Chicken Soup for the Soul, Cup of Comfort* and *Guideposts*. He also covets the faithful encouragement of his wife, Geri, and children Rebekah and Matthew. He writes to bless God's children. Contact David at davidandgeri@hotmail.com.

Kristin Caraway Whitaker—Kris was born in El Paso, Texas, and has enjoyed living in many other places during her lifetime. She credits the interesting locations and many wonderful friends she has made in each place with helping her adjust to the many moves and changes along the way. Most recently she has spent two years in Okinawa, Japan, and is now living with her husband and their beloved cat in Schonaich, a small village near Stuttgart, Germany. Once the editor of her small town newspaper, the *Leader Journal* in St. James, Missouri, Kristin is now enjoying semi-retirement in Germany. She still writes stories and poems for 11 grandchildren and others, and takes many photos of the great places that she and husband, Randy, visit every chance they get. She can be reached by e-mail at randyw20@att.net.

Catherine L. Young—Cat is a technology teacher, Toastmaster, writer, and a board member of the St. Davids Christian Writers Association. An avid learner, she develops her writing skills at the annual St. Davids Chrisitain Writers' Conference and Delmarva Christian Writers' Fellowship. Cat has been published multiple times in *Penned from the Heart* and can be reached at cyoungsvt@gmail.com.

Our Advent Book

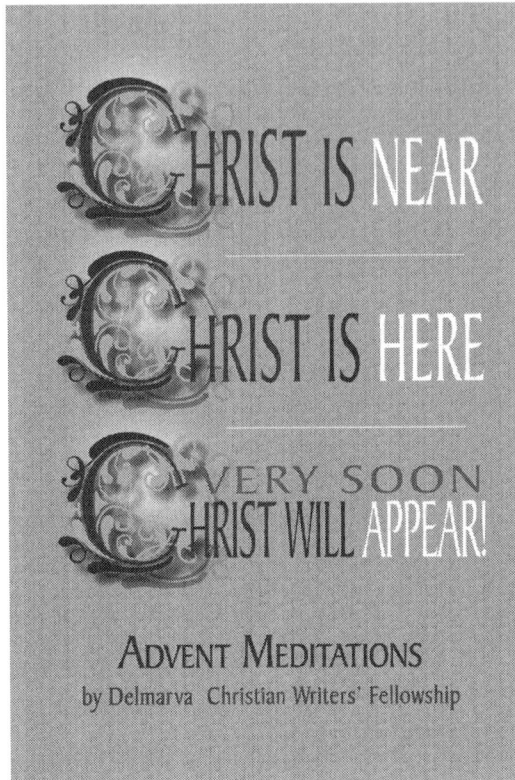

CHRIST IS NEAR

CHRIST IS HERE

VERY SOON CHRIST WILL APPEAR!

ADVENT MEDITATIONS
by Delmarva Christian Writers' Fellowship

CHRIST IS NEAR: Advent Meditations by Delmarva Christian Writers' Fellowship, was initially published in 2002 to give beginning writers an opportunity to see their work in print. Completely revised and re-released in 2011, this 36-page booklet offers devotions from the first Sunday in Advent through Christmas Day. It is available from Amazon.com.

CHRIS✝MAS

This book is available on Amazon.com.

For autographed copies
or for information on
Delmarva Christian Writers' Fellowship
Visit www.DelmarvaWriters.com

Candy Abbott
Fruitbearer Publishing, LLC
P. O. Box 777
Georgetown, DE 19947
302.856.6649
302.856.7742 (fax)
info@fruitbearer.com

Made in the USA
Charleston, SC
22 November 2012